The Extraordinary Life of an Ordinary Man
(1912 – 2018)

Written by George Harold Clough
Edited by Mavis, Mark and Charlotte Clarkson

Chapters

Foreword

Not many people can say they have had the pleasure of meeting their great-grandfather; let alone being able to say they have met a man who has lived to the ripe old age of one hundred and five.

Fortunately, I am one of the lucky few. My great-grandfather – Gramps, to me – was born in a mining town in the early twentieth century, the second son of Sam and Ethel Clough. In his one hundred and five years, he lived life to the fullest. Although he was not wealthy in the financial sense, he considered himself rich beyond measures – with a large, happy family, span of different and fulfilling careers and over a hundred years' worth of love and laughter.

In celebration of his wonderful life, we have edited this book of his memories; not only do they detail the extraordinary life of an ordinary man, but the changing of twentieth century Britain.

For my Gramps: George Harold Clough (27.12.1912 – 16.05.2018)

Charlotte Clarkson
May 2018

I find it hard at my age to look back and remember the happenings of my life, but I shall endeavour to share a few of my many memories with you. So, as they say, let's start at the very beginning...

I was born in Worsborough, an area of Barnsley in South Yorkshire, on 27th November 1912; a notably snowy winter for the north of England as I was told. I was the second child of Sam and Ethel (née Darnborough) Clough, my brother Willie being only eighteen months older.

We were a good, working-class family, living on the fringes of northern poverty in twentieth century England. A jam jar as a mug, a canal as a swimming pool, we made do with what we had, and we did it with a smile on our faces.

I don't remember much of my earlier years, though I can say for certain I was not fortunate enough to know the luxuries the youths seem to enjoy today. In fact, one of my earliest of recollections is of the Great War, during which time I was only a babe. As the War raged across Europe, our small family had gone to live with an Aunt in the small village of Measboro' Dyke. I recall being taken from my bed during the night and being carried into the cold night air, up a mound what I later came to know as the Hilly Fields.

Willie and I were told to keep quiet as we saw a Zeppelin flying overhead. In times of air-raids, it seemed most people within the locality evacuated to the Hilly Fields as industrialised areas such as Barnsley were targeted by the Germans.

Whenever I thought about this afterwards, I thought that we went to the Hilly Fields because it was above the town and therefore, we had a better view of what my innocent mind saw as huge, cigar-shaped airship. But in actual fact it was for our own safety, for these roaring Zeppelins carried bombs.

I do not remember much else of my time living with my Aunt, as my small family would move only a short while later from Measboro' Dyke to Stairfoot, a little over a mile away. It was in this village I was to spend the next sixteen or seventeen years of my life; and where our small family would increase from four to fourteen – not so small anymore!

Number 12, Albion Road was to become our new home. I must mention before I go on that this street and the street stretching along beside it, Industry Road, had developed the nickname Sodom! Why? I suppose I shall never know, because the people were no worse than others to bring such a name upon the area, and as I read the current newspapers, it seems to me that such an epithet could be applied to most places today! However, despite its nickname, I found mostly kindliness and neighbourliness outstanding and although much poverty abounded, there was always a sharing of the little that we had. Such good memories I have of my time there.

The houses along Albion Road were back-to-back terrace houses; meaning there were other houses attached to the back of the house and to either side of it and only one singular entrance from the street to each home. We lived in the front of the street, in a row of about twenty houses.

Our home on Albion Road was rather large; the houses were three storeys, plus a cellar. In our home, the living room and kitchen were combined, with one bedroom, an attic and a cellar with a pantry at the top of the cellar stairs.

The living room was lit by gas and was always quite bright when the mantle was good – which wasn't very often! The gas was laid into the bedroom, but as it was simply a bracket sticking out from the wall with no fitting to attach a mantle, only a small blue flame could be seen. As for the attic, well, we just had to manage with a candle... like I said, we made do with what we had!

Being so poor, our flooring in the living room was simply flagstones and, without carpets, one can almost feel how cold it was to the bare feet, though we always had quite a few homemade rugs spread around, with a large one down by the hearth.

I recall making the rugs very well as it was a hobby Dad enjoyed very much. We had a large frame in the living room on which the canvas was stretched to allow him to trace patterns; this meant those of us who liked to help would know where to put the coloured clippings of fabric. I remember him cutting up the cloth to the required lengths with a special pair of scissors, I was fascinated by the dexterity he displayed when doing this, as the clippings hardly varied in length. I often wonder what happened to those scissors, as I know he prized them very much.

One item I did get which belonged to him was the last[1] he would use to mend his own boots and shoes; as you can probably assume, my Dad was a bit of a mender, but you had to be in those days. He was quite good at it as well and kept himself busy with the needs of his own family, as well as his neighbours. It was hard to get leather in those days since we had such a little money, but Dad always made do with what he had and often he would put cardboard soles into shoes when they were riddled with holes and there wasn't enough money for the leather. Years ago, I made pretty good use of the last myself and became quite proficient at it. I suppose it wasn't entirely a waste when I watched him as a youngster!

With only rugs for carpet and candles for light, one can well imagine that we did not have the luxury of running water in our 'palace' at 12 Albion Road. For hot water, we relied upon the oven, keeping a bucket filled with water in the oven by the fire whenever we weren't cooking. This meant we always had hot water for getting washed with.

It was definitely difficult to keep clean in those days, especially as Dad and later my brother and I were miners, and therefore were working in the filthiest of conditions. Our tin bath certainly came in handy after spending hours underground! We kept it on a hook in the kitchen and on bath nights, it would be filled with hot water and placed in front of the fire. On those days I was most thankful for the oven and bucket!

Of course, it was a hard job filling the bath and the water wouldn't stay warm for too long, so Mum and Dad enjoyed the luxury first, then us children. Because it took such a good while to fill the bath, this procedure was a once a week job. In between, us miners struggled since there were no washing facilities at work, instead hoping a good wash in between shifts would keep us as dirt-free as possible. It probably seems unbelievable to you now, when everyone has bathrooms with baths and showers, but we managed and thought nothing about it because back in those days it was the norm.

As the family grew with Mum's constant pregnancies, we children (particularly the girls in those days) were expected to help, and I found myself quite domesticated in my childhood; from washing dishes, helping with the cooking and even donkey-stoning[2] the steps. Often, I would join the girls in helping with the housework – cooking and cleaning

---

[1] Last - used by cobblers when mending shoes. It is made from cast iron and shaped tripod like on three different sized feet. The cobbler chooses which is the best size foot for the shoe he is mending, places the shoe on this so that it is on the top of the last and the last rests on the other two feet. This enables the cobbler to have his hands free to work on the shoe.

[2] Donkey-stoning – steps and ledges would be washed with water and then coloured with a white or yellow ochre donkey-stone.

had to be done before playing out – however my brother, Willie felt housework was not his role. Remember, this was an age where men went to work, and women looked after the house.

I treasure fond memories of our house on 12 Albion Road being filled with delicious smells on baking day as the girls would prance around the kitchen helping Mum as soon as they were old enough. The Clough speciality on baking day was a 'Ston o bread[3]', mainly because it lasted a few days and was made with meagre ingredients. Back then, the most important thing was how much you could make with the little you had, especially when you had fourteen mouths to feed.

Anyhow, now I have described what life was like within our home on Albion Road, I must tell you of the outside. The structure of the back-to-back houses on Albion Road relied upon a ginnel which gave those of us who lived at the front houses, access to the back and vice-versa. Our home was situated approximately halfway between the top of the street and the ginnel, meaning whichever way we went to get to the back, it was much the same distance – about three or four hundred yards. To you, this may not seem unfortunate, but I can assure you, the prospect of travelling to the back in order to use the closet during wintry nights (or days, for that matter) was not a pleasant one.

Our closet at 12 Albion Road, more commonly known as a toilet these days, was not attached to our home but was situated at the back of the row of houses. They were all earth closets, with two cold metal barrels fixed over a hole in the ground with twin wooden seats attached across the top of it, designed for the use of more than one family.

We shared our closet with the people living immediately behind us, and when I think of it, the entry door to their home was only a few yards away from the midden[4], so one can well imagine the smell when the closets were emptied.

During the day, two men came around our streets on a horse and cart to empty the toilets, armed with long shovels which they used to remove all the debris from below. When the closets were cleared, disinfectant powder was scattered all about in an attempt to supress the stench, however I must say that on these particular occasions, I was always very thankful our house was situated in the front of the street.

I do recall a rather uncouth rhyme that we children would follow these men and sing whilst they emptied our closets:

'My old man's a Middy Man[5]
He shovels for his bit[6]
Sometimes he shovels loads of muck
And others, loads of s***!'

Although these closets were largely unsanitary and not exactly pleasant, we were happy to make do, as was everybody else. You see, inside toilets were almost unheard of in

---

[3] Ston o bread - stone of bread, a stone was fourteen pounds. To make a stone of bread a stone of flour was used.

[4] Midden – a waste piece of ground where people used to tip their rubbish, usually ashes from the fire. There was a grid on the ground which allowed the ashes to go through and onto the ground below, where the earth closets were dug out.

[5] Middy Man – a dustbin man employed by the council who would often see to clearing out the debris from the earth closets.

[6] Bit – a slang term for a person's wages.

those days unless you were very rich, so at night, rather than going down to the street to the closet, we would use a chamber pot. This was a round container with a handle that was placed beneath the bed, ready for use during the night, and then taken down the street to be emptied in the morning. In truth, chamber pots cost money, and for us, it was cheaper to use a bucket.

Those more fortunate than us had tippler toilets. The exterior of these lavatories was identical to our own earth closets but were much deeper inside the 'pan'. A hole was dug about five feet beneath the toilet seat with a container placed beneath. When said container was full, it would tip up and empty into the sewer whilst water from the sink would empty into this container to flush the tippler.

Despite all I say, I do recall some comical memories of these toilets. On very cold, dark nights, a couple of us boys would go together, taking matches with us and set light to the paper scattered among the ashes below (no toilet paper in those days!) and have, what was described as a 'warm sitting'.

My happy memories of Stairfoot are not, however, limited to these nights during my years as a young boy. I do recall a piece of waste ground at the bottom of my road and just beyond it, the canal on which coal barges, pulled by horses would travel. We spent happy times in the fields around the canal and, though it was strictly forbidden, many brilliant memories were made within the canal itself. Every so often, it was discovered of our bathing within the canal waters and after a few good hidings, it suddenly dawned on us – Willie and I – how Mum and Dad knew we had been in the canal. And so, never again did we swim in the canal unless we had had a good wash at home beforehand, and it just so happened that we were never caught again! Such happy days they were, especially in the summertime, going for a swim, and then running around the field until we were dry enough to put our clothes back on.

Another treat during my childhood was a visit to the pictures at Barnsley's 'Flea Pit' or 'Bug House' as we called it. This cost a penny a time. The favourites of those days were Pearl White and Eddie Pola, featuring in serials lasting about twelve or thirteen weeks. I remember one day a few of us setting off to go the pictures, and halfway to Barnsley we stopped to have a game of Roly Poly down a hill known as Monument Field, with its gentle slope. Unfortunately, while rolling down the field repeatedly, most of us lost our coppers out of our pockets and so, had to return home without so much as a glimpse of the pictures.

However, less happy times were to come... Stairfoot was a mining area, and in those days the pits were not doing so well. People were only working two or three days a week, so many men found themselves with quite a lot of time to spare. Many of them had allotments[7] where they spent their time tending to plants, others, especially the younger miners, played games. Apart from the usual football and cricket, they played Handball, Bounceball or Nipsy alongside us children.

Handball and Bounceball were played by using the wall of an end terrace house. A thick chalk line was drawn across the length of the wall, about three feet from the ground and the objective of the game was to hit the ball with the palm of the hand and knock it against the wall above the chalk line (otherwise it was a point lost), the first player to reach eleven points was crowned the winner. I must say I have seen some great games,

---

[7] Allotments – a plot of land where people could grow flowers or vegetables. These were usually rented from the council, as very few people had gardens attached to their houses in those days.

with rallies taking quite some time before one or the other of the players missed the wall or played under the chalk line.

The game required little skill, but much energy and one must not forget the rough ground and the need for pretty hard hands when playing either Handball or Bounceball.

Looking back, I suppose it was a form of modern-day squash, only without racquets in our case. And perhaps with heftier consequences... as I must mention it was always best, if possible, to organise a game while the occupants of the house were out as people did not take kindly to soot falling down the chimney when the balls were to hit just the right spot.

As for the game of Nipsy (or Knur and Spell, to give it its proper name), it was played with a round piece of wood, the hardest that one could get, approximately three inches long and about one and a half inches in diameter, with one end shaped into a point. This was placed onto a raised, flat stone. Then, armed with a pick handle, the trick was to touch the piece of wood lightly on the point so that it rose into the air and, before it could fall, give it a mighty whack to send the Nipsy as far away as possible.

It was then that the person who had hit the Nipsy would estimate how many strides his opponent would need to take to reach it - a kind of hop, stride, and jump effort. If he managed to reach the objective in the estimated number of strides, he won. In my time I have seen quite a bit of money change hands when players were not so lucky to have won, as was the case with most games played by the miners.

Living in a mining village, it was a common occurrence for boys to leave schooling to work down in the pits, as Willie and I were to do whilst living in Stairfoot. Up until the age of fourteen when I left education for work, school days, as I remember them, were quite enjoyable, though I must say they were rather interrupted as the family was increased almost each year.

Being the most domesticated of the boys, I found myself at home quite a lot, helping with the chores. However, I do recall being invited into a class, coaching to sit for the scholarship for entrance into the nearby Grammar School, just a few weeks before 'sitting'.

I passed for the Grammar School, but due to our circumstances, I went to the ordinary senior school in Barnsley. You see, my parents couldn't afford for me to go with the expense of the uniform and books and, I would have had to leave when I reached the age of fourteen, for working life anyway.

Whilst I speak of the Grammar School, I must mention that I happened to be away from school just before the summer break and was unable to attend the headmaster announcing the names of the scholarship winners, though I do know that, when coming to my name he put in a little aside: 'If he attends the next school as much as he's attended this one, he won't be attending much.' My only comment is that I must have made good use of the time I spent there. Mind you, I didn't want to stay away from school, it was simply a force of circumstances that kept me away.

I recall walking to and from school on the days I was able to attend – a good two miles each way – sometimes, coming home for dinner as well, but more often than not it was cheaper to take sandwiches. This was mostly bread and dripping[8], or if there wasn't any dripping, bread and lard would suffice. Sometimes, when finances were a little better, it became a treat to take a penny into the Fish and Chip tent at the market in Barnsley

---

[8] Dripping – the fat left after a joint of meat had been cooked.

and have a side of chips with my sandwiches. It seems ridiculous today to talk of taking a penny and asking for a half-penny worth of each, but really it was a luxury to be able to do it in those days. Normally, finances were not so good, especially with the mining strikes ravaging Stairfoot. Because of this, the children in our streets used to be breakfasted in the chapel schoolrooms at the top of the street. We were given bread and margarine and mug of cocoa when our parents couldn't afford to feed us, let alone spoil us with fish and chips for lunch. In fact, I recall one morning in 1921 going for breakfast at the schoolrooms and finding myself next to a lad who had two thumbs on one of his hands. At nine years old, I was quite fascinated by this, although it did put me off my breakfast and so I went to school hungry that day.

Days at the Central School in Barnsley were quite good, although coming from poor circumstances; I – like many others – was somewhat disadvantaged regarding school clothes and bus fares. Nevertheless, in those days one learned to cope and didn't complain much about things, though times were very, very hard...

I don't want to feel sorry for myself but Stairfoot truly was pillaged by poverty, and yet it seemed things were looking up for the neighbouring Barnsley. As we struggled day in and day out for the necessities, Barnsley was enjoying the innovations of Charabangs[9] and Trackies[10]. Yet, despite all these innovations so close to home, life was much the same for us with a shortage of money due to the pit strikes.

Some days we didn't know where the next meal was coming from, and I remember often sitting beside the firelight with an aching belly, as we hadn't a penny to put in the gas meter. Maybe you will wonder at having fuel for the fire but no money for the gas! Well, if the supply of coal from the colliery had run out (this was the amount of coal each miner received as part of their wages) and the next was overdue, then one borrowed from a neighbour, or alternatively, went to the muck tip picking bits of coal from the dross and waste that came out of the pit.

We always called them slag heaps. Huge mountains of coals dust, rubble and chunks to be seen near every pit. Of course, as children we were forbidden to play on them, but that never seemed to stop us, and quite filthy states we would be in, as you can imagine. We got scolded something horrible, and if the watchman were to see us playing there, he would chase us, only adding to the fun of this miner's playground. Mind you, he never actually managed to catch us either!

As a child, I used to think it was out of sheer malice that we were forbidden from playing on the slag heaps, but of course these heaps were a dangerous playground for children. However, despite it being against the rules, if we had no coal that's where we would go to scavenge for some good chunks, anything you could light a fire with at home. Anything was better than nothing.

Of course, we weren't the only family to do this. Stairfoot was a poor town and all the neighbour's children did the same when times were tough. If we had been caught, I'm sure we would have been in quite some trouble, as I suppose it was classed as thieving, but I don't recall anybody ever being caught. Sometimes the consequences of doing without was far scarier than the risk of 'forgetting' the law.

I remember on one such occasion when we were struggling, Dad and Willie had gone to the Barrow Colliery to pick some coal for the fires at home. Willie wondered too

---

[9] Charabangs – a form of transport; similar to a tram, Charabangs had four or five rows of seats, each holding six people with separate doors to each row.
[10] Trackies – slang term for buses as they did not run on rails like trams or trains.

close to a part of the stack that was burning and was overcome by the fumes. Fortunately, Dad saw him just as he collapsed and hurried to get him away from the danger zone. Perhaps my brother was simply accident prone as I recall another time during my infancy when he swallowed an open safety pin which naturally caused some anxiety within the family. It took one or two visits to the hospital before the Doctors were satisfied that he has parted with it naturally. Even with that in mind, I'm still not convinced Willie's daring nature or his susceptibility to accidents was at fault for his close encounter with death on that day wandering the slag heap with Dad.

Years later in 1966, the whole world learned how dangerous these slag heaps were – my childhood playground – when one engulfed a school in the village of Aberfan in Wales, killing 116 children and 28 adults. The tragedy was caused by a water build up after a lot of rainfall in the huge slag heap above the village, causing it to slide down the hillside.

Since the closure of the coal mines under Thatcher's government, these black coal hills have been landscaped into the lush green countryside, and the miner's playgrounds are no more. It certainly reminds me of the differences between the world I grew up in and the world we live in now.

Coal was not the only thing my family would often have to struggle for days without; some days fourteen mouths were simply too many to feed. On those days, when finances were not so well, we relied upon the cheaper foods available.

I remember many a Saturday night when my sister, Linda and I were sent to the market as it was closing to buy the produce they were selling at as cheap a price as we children could haggle. More often than not, we would get meat and vegetables at half the cost and the family would be treated to the first nourishing meal in weeks.

My favourite meal was our Sunday morning breakfast, as Dad was quite the chef when he set his mind to it, which was unusual, for men didn't often do things around the house in those days. I remember sitting together for our breakfast dinner for years, enjoying the stew Dad would make from the scraps of meat and vegetables we bartered for the night before.

Dad really was quite the cook, and a real dab hand[11] at making Yorkshire Puddings. It was always his job to make these whenever we were having a roast dinner. As children, we always had our fill of Yorkshire Puddings and gravy before the rest of the meal. This was done so that we filled up on the cheaper food to make sure there was enough dinner to go around all of us. In fact, I remember one Sunday my Aunt Mary arrived unexpectedly with her family and, of course, Mum and Dad were worried that there wouldn't be enough food to feed us all. *'Don't worry, Sam,'* was my Aunt's response, *'We've only come for your Yorkshire Puddings and gravy!'*.

I remember Dad was also quite talented at making Bees Wine. The 'plant' was kept in the kitchen on the windowsill, and if memory serves me well, it was a mixture of water, black treacle and sugar which fermented as it aged. The plant was fed weekly in what quantities I don't know, but the liquid was poured off and bottled. It never lasted very long, as it was drunk fairly quickly so I don't know if it had a long shelf life. Years later in the 1950's we did a similar thing with what we called a Ginger Beer plant. My Dad was fond of his drink and his Bees Wine was very sweet and slightly alcoholic. Because of its sweetness, the plants liquid was diluted to make the drink. As I said earlier, Sodom was

---

[11] Dab hand – proficient.

a neighbourhood of sharing and each week the liquid was drained, the plant would be halved and the plant extract was put in a glass and taken to a neighbour, ready to feed and start a new one for the next week. At one time, I dare say half of Sodom was drunk from my Dad's little 'plant'.

Thinking of Dad making Bees Wine reminds me of Popalol, the drink we youngsters used to make. We would break up hard Spanish[12] and put into an empty pop bottle, fill it with water and shake it up vigorously. It would then be left for the Spanish to dissolve into the liquid. Providing the shaker was good at their job, we children would have a tasty and cheap drink. In those days we didn't have much money for sweets, but sometimes Mum would give us a small stick of rhubarb and a bit of sugar; we would dip the rhubarb in the sugar and eat that. Still quite sour, but as children we enjoyed the treat. Other times, she would give us a wrapping of cocoa and sugar mixed together for us to dip our fingers into, looking back it was a sort of homemade khali or sherbet sweet.

Speaking of Mum reminds of her excellent cooking skills. Whilst Dad reigned over with his Yorkshire Puddings, Mum's speciality was a huge pan of Corned Beef Hash. This mainly consisted of a few slices of corned beef bought from the shop at the end of our street, *The Globe*, and then, loads of potatoes and a few carrots and onions (if we could get them) were added to the mixture. She served this dished up onto the top of a thick pancake, again, filling food with a bit of nourishment.

Whilst I speak of the matter, I must commend my parents for their work in the kitchen, during a time of no electrical toasters or ovens with grills. In those days, we had a long brass fork called a toasting fork; we would put bread on the prongs of the fork and hold it over the fire to toast it, and then turn it over to do the other side. I must say, the soot and inevitable burnt bits when it fell into the fire, simply added to the flavour.

Talking of this reminds me that we were not just poor, but I was, in fact, brought up under the hard hands of poverty. Our diet was very poor and although Mum would always try her best with what she had, it would become harder and harder as the family grew and grew. Often, she would rely on the corner shop for her ingredients and would pay by tick[13]; we would get things and pay for them at the end of the week on pay day. It put food on the table and into our bellies, but this never-ending vicious cycle would only start over again the following week.

My dear old Dad was not especially helpful in our situation either. He wasn't much of a drinker (although he did enjoy a pint or two) but unfortunately, he was a gambler. If he went to Barnsley before taking his wage packet home, it would often mean that he would gamble the lot and leave Mum and the kids with no money for the week. Finances were bad as it was, but without Dad's pay packet there was no money for the bills or the food for the week. Often, Linda and I would go to meet Dad on the day he got his wages, sitting outside the pub and waiting for him in the hopes of stopping him from catching the bus to Barnsley and ensuring our lifeline for the week. On one such occasion we were not so lucky, and Mum was furious with him. She was so angry with Dad that she burnt all of his photographs, consequently we only have two or three photos of him now. In spite of all this, my Dad was not a bad father, in many ways he was very good, just prone to mistakes as we all can be.

---

[12] Spanish – a Yorkshire slang term for liquorice.
[13] Tick – on credit.

Of course, no wages were a large issue for our even larger family. No weekly wage meant that anything decent we had, which usually wasn't very much would go to the pawn shop. The pawn shop was on our street; a shop at the front and a pawn shop at the back. If someone was going around the back of the shop you could imagine how they were struggling. We pawned a lot of our things, which meant that we were given money for something and a ticket. With that, we had a length of time in which we could redeem our things by returning the ticket with the required money to the pawn shop. Anything we had for our 'Sunday best' was the first to be pawned, and that is why we always had to take such good care of our best things, so that we could get the best price for them.

That being said, a lot of us children were not so lucky to have our own 'Sunday best' clothes as we always wore hand-me-downs. In fact, I rarely remember getting anything new as a child although I must admit our family was fortunate at having a mender as a father.

However, I'm happy to say that it was not entirely a time of woe for my family as I do recall some rather lovely memories with my Dad. The first was when I was about five years old, my younger brother Harry had just been born and my mother was bedridden. It was a Saturday dinnertime just before Christmas and I went up to the street to meet my Dad after work. As it was both pay day and Christmas time, he had been celebrating a little too much and when I saw him staggering down the hill at the top of the street I ran towards him, feverish with anxiety and pushed him up the wall crying *'Tha'll tumble down Daddy, don't move!'*. Needless to say, he couldn't move because, besides being a little drunk, he was helpless with laughter.

Another recollection concerning my Dad happened at Christmastime only a few years later. Again, he had had some liquid refreshment and decided to liven things up a little and spread some festive spirit across Sodom. He took the gramophone horn from our home, went out into the cold street and began singing through it. I must say, he was quite a good singer too (as was Mum) and it sounded terrific to us children and delighted the neighbours who thought it had been the best Christmas up to date. Mum was not so fond of Dad's Christmas jigging and soon put a stop to it.

Speaking of Christmas reminds me of all the wonderful holidays we enjoyed in Stairfoot. Oh, our holidays at Albion Road were ever so memorable! A highlight of those days was Whitsuntide, as on the Monday of the holiday, all the local chapels with the Sunday school scholars would parade down the streets carrying their various banners, led by a Brass Band. This was known as the 'Whit Walk' and, at the end of this walk, we all congregated in a local field for food and organised games of sport.

A particular speciality of Whitsuntide was that no matter how poor the people were, most of the children had new clothes to wear on the walk. It did not matter that a lot of them were taken to the pawnshop afterwards as it did not take away the joy of the memorable day. Strangely enough, when I look back to those days, I cannot remember a single rainy Whit Monday. I suppose it is because one tends to remember the good things in life, as it should be.

It is true that poverty and misfortune were in real abundance among the families of Stairfoot in my childhood but despite all the difficulties we faced, I will always look back fondly on those days of my youth. Oh, what a different world we lived in.

From back left, Willie and I, with Linda, Harry and Ann. It was not unusual at the time for boys to wear dresses in their infancy, up until the age of two years.

Sam at centre back. Dad's family before his marriage with his Mum, Dad and siblings at the end of the nineteenth century. Note the Victorian clothing at this time.

From left, Kathleen, Bernard and Annie. Three more of my siblings.

Mum with the twins, Dennis and Daisy.

A photo of my Mum, Ethel, in later life.

It was just after the coal strike in 1926 that I started my working life. At the age of thirteen, I left school one day and started work at Mitchell Main the next, my fourteenth birthday.

On that day, picture me rising at half past four in the morning and, after a pot of tea and a slice of bread and dripping, setting off with my brother and a few other lads on the two-mile walk through the cold November morning to the pit. On arrival we were directed to the lamp room to be given a check with a number stamped on (I recall my check read 542) and having been given the lamp – they were mostly oil lamps in those days – we joined the procession of boys and men making their way to the pit head.

What a sight – all those lights gleaming in the dark mornings! It certainly was a vast difference to the previous morning as I wended my way to school for the last time; little did I know there were far greater eye openers in store for me…

I was equipped in the essential items of clothing for the miners of my days, with a waistcoat, specially altered with large homemade pockets on the inside to hold a quart bottle of water each. In the districts far from the pit bottom, it was very hot and sticky, and the water was not only appreciated but needed. To save time and energy with extra journeys, men would often take three waistcoats at a time. Just imagine that, me, fourteen years old, slung with three waistcoats on my back, each with two-quart bottles of water in and often, on top of that, a tin of Dudley. Staggering along, bent almost double, what a funny thing to imagine now.

As we climbed the steps, we approached the cage[14] with a man stationed along beside it; we were each searched thoroughly to ensure no man had left matches or cigarettes in their pockets, if so, they were confiscated. After this search, at last, I clambered into the cage despite my trepidation. I was joined by about nine other men in my cage, and the same amount in the one attached below before the gates were drawn closed and the bell clanged. The cage lifted a little to allow the fallers to be removed and whoosh, down we went. I remember the feeling of my stomach rising into my mouth as we dropped for miles until gradually, the falling seemed to steady, and we arrived at the pit bottom.

As I write this, I must say, that once we miners stepped on the cage and went plunging downwards, we were cut off from the sun, the stars, the moon and the fresh air – all things that one takes for granted – we were literally buried alive for eight hours or so, but one got used to it, and living in a colliery district one had to, so for the next few years such was my life and I like many others did not complain I resigned myself to the fact and was happy with my lot in life.

The pit bottom itself was surprising and shocking; an amazing revelation as to my new subterranean workplace. I gazed at the high arched roofs interspersed with electric lighting. In the pit bottom an individual's oil lamp was surplus to requirements and were therefore hung on protruding nails hammered into the pit walls.

Having arrived at the pit bottom, we each handed our check in at the check hole. Here, they were placed onto a board, ready to be collected at the end of the shift. Once collected they were returned to the lamp hole on arrival at the pit top.

---

[14] Cage – a sort of lift to take people from one floor of the mine to another.

My first job in the mines was known as 'dragging chains'. Explaining it now may seem rather confusing to some of you: chains were used to haul full tubs of coal from the various districts into the workshop, when the full tubs arrived at the pit bottom, the chains were uncoupled from the tubs and placed on top of the coal. When these tubs reached the cage it was my job to pull the chains off of the top of the coal and drag them around to the other side of the cage, where empty tubs were being sorted and assembled in readiness to be hauled to the level end and despatched once more to the workings. This work was very strenuous and heavy and one's hands were quite numb with the cold, but it was a discomfort that had to be endured.

I remember exactly how I felt by the end of that long, long day. In a matter of hours, my whole world had been transformed, forsaking the relative comforts of a school classroom

The work at Mitchell Main Colliery was hard, not just for me but for the poor animals used back in those days. After my work dragging the chains, the empty tubs were taken to the level end from the pit bottom by ponies; however, at Mitchell Main Colliery cart horses were used because the roof space was so high. During my time at Mitchell Main, there were two cart horses named Jolly and Jerry.

It wasn't long before I became a cart horse driver, working with Jolly to take the empty tubs with the spare chains to the level end to be attached to the endless rope in the main place and then conveyed to the districts further in the mine. A giant patchwork of ropes interspersed with tubs, their wooden carcasses formed around an iron sub-frame designed to receive and carry the freshly hewn coal, its tentacles circumnavigating the farthest reaches of the working coal mine.

After a while spent working in the pit bottom fulfilling the role of 'Driver'[15] I became adept at harnessing and unharnessing the cart horses. Jolly and I had developed a fondness to each other and at the end of the shift I would take Jolly back to the stables. These were situated just off the pit bottom. Once I'd stabled my 'own' horse Jolly, I used to wait for my brother, Willie who worked down 4th North, a district about four miles from the pit bottom.

Nip[16] and I had always been attached, being so close in age and working alongside one another in the mines. During those days I looked up to him and depended on him a great deal. After all, he had twelve months experience behind him in his mining work and in my naïve young eyes seemed like quite the veteran. I remember how he would come bursting into the stables and take his horse, Toby into his stall. He would take off Toby's harness and Toby, as if glad to be free of it, used to give his head a vigorous shake. Each and every time, Nip would come flying headlong out of the stall; picking himself up he used to say *'You'd think I would have learned to avoid that by now after driving him for so long.'* Oh, how he did make me chuckle.

Willie was always a great source of comfort to me during my days as a miner. I remember one such occasion, on arriving to work I was told that I was required to work down 5th North, the last district in the pit and about four and a half miles from the pit bottom. To say I was nervous would be an understatement and it seemed an endless journey to me. But with Nip and Toby as reassuring companions on their way to 4th North,

---

[15] Driver – the person in charge of a pit poney or cart horse.
[16] Nip – an interchangeable nickname between the two brothers, Harold and Willie.

I felt much more at ease. I still recall the horse I was to drive on this journey. He was a black horse called Smut with a single white spot on the end of his nose.

On this shift, I remember leaving the stables and passing through about three lots of air doors. Before you could open each door, you had to operate a slide set in the middle of the door. The airway was cruel on my young lungs; all the time you spent going to your work area you were faced by a constant flow of warm air from the fan, it was stifling. It was like the feeling you get on opening an oven and being 'hit' by the heat emanating from the working appliance. This was compounded by a perpetual cloud of dust that hung in the air, stirred up by foot traffic from the men, boys and ponies all going to the different districts in which they worked, 1st North, 2nd North and so on up to the 5th North where I was bound.

After 4 miles, Nip and Toby peeled off to go to their workplace at 4th North and for the last half mile or so of our journey, Smut and I traversed the main plane where the tubs – both empty and full – were lashed on to an endless steel rope that was continually in motion. Conditions changed as we entered the main plane; it was in stark contrast to the return airway tunnel as the stifling temperature dropped and was replaced by refreshing, fresh and cool air.

Eventually I arrived at 5th North. Even now, the only words I can think to describe the scenes are reminiscent of *Dante's Inferno*[17]. I was confronted with a multitude of near naked bodies, rivulets of sweat streaming down their flesh and pooling in their scant clothes. It was unbearably hot, eyes glowing like smouldering coal, almost emerging from their blackened faces, the ponies dripping sweat too. Frankly I would have gone back to school right away after that sight, little did I know there would be worse to come...

In 5th North, the high vaulted roof of the pit bottom was long gone, replaced with a roof so low that one had to walk in most places with a stoop. After knocking my head a few times, I soon learned to keep it down. The reason the roof was so low was because this was the area where the coal was being mined and extracted, we referred to it as 'the workings'.

I can only describe my first experience of graft in the workings to be a waking nightmare. Being a youngster of fourteen, I can well imagine how nervous I was and how this trepidation will not have helped the shift run smoother however, even now, I shiver at the memory of that dreaded place.

Firstly, Smut wasn't such a tractable pony as Jolly was, but he was unquestionably made worse than usual in sensing my nervousness and newness. Secondly, I was left on a level on my own, a little way from the other half a dozen or so drivers, which didn't help. In spite of this, I set off to do my work with a couple of empty tubs and managed to reach the place where the two miners had two full tubs ready to exchange.

With two full tubs in tow, I set off for the level end but unfortunately, Smut had other ideas planned and didn't want to pull the full tubs. In my efforts to try and encourage movement, I stumbled in the poorly lit tunnel and the sudden jolt put my oil lamp out. Talk about darkness, I could feel it swallowing me up and I was very thankful for Smut's lack of movement in that moment, otherwise I would have been in a real mess. It wasn't long before I'd gotten myself into a bit of a panic. I remember shouting myself hoarse for what seemed like hours. Eventually, the Corporal[18] came to my rescue and

---

[17] *Dante's Inferno* – a fourteenth century epic poem 'Divine Comedy' where the author journey's through Hell.

[18] Corporal – the man in charge of a certain mining district and therefore is in charge of the district's drivers

escorted me to the level end where my lamp was re-lit, but it wasn't long before I was plunged back into the darkness, armed with only my little oil lamp again.

Like tales of blind men, I found my other senses would become more focussed in times of struggle when lamps had failed, or candles blown during my shifts in 5th North. Later on, that same shift, there I was again, lamp-less and straining my eyes in the hopes of spotting the glimmer of another man's lamp. Listening to the exaggerated sounds from around me, bits of roof falling, timbers creaking, mice scurrying around. Even with hindsight in mind, I can tell you I was really frightened. All I could do was sit it out and wait. Time passed by so slowly in these hours.

To say I was happy for the end of that shift would be a trifle understated. We retraced our earlier steps and on approaching the entrance to 4th North and hearing the voice of our Nip, I could have jumped for joy. The dulcet tones of a miner singing 'Moonlight and Roses', a very popular song of the day, could be heard before he could be seen. Nonchalantly, singing away with Toby by his side, waiting for his Nip.

I truly found this first day in 'the workings' to be a baptism of fire, deep in the bowels of Barnsley's coal seam. However, all things come to an end, as thankfully did my first shift there. After that, it didn't take me long to get used to the darkness and if I found myself in such a predicament again, I soon learned to bend down and feel for the rail and, in doing so, would work my way along it until reaching the relative safety of a manhole[19].

The next day at Mitchell Main, I stayed in the pit bottom and did so for a while after that until eventually I was recruited to work down 3rd North. This district was called Billingley, because it was situated underneath the village of Billingley, some seven miles to the east of Barnsley.

Whilst here, again, I was a pony driver, responsible for ten men. There were 'holes', each with three men working in them and one 'hole' with four men. My job was to keep them supplied with empty tubs and bring them out when full. I tell you now, it was hectic work and one hardly had time to eat ones snap[20]; I would just about uncork my bottle and bite at a sandwich when the Corporal would holler, 'Come on Harold, there are other drivers who want to eat besides thee,'.

Now that I think of it, it seems a lot of my time spent working the mines was filled with worry and terror. One thing that sent a chill down one's spine whilst working down the pit was the word 'runner', a term used to describe a set of tubs hurtling down an incline under their own momentum, caused by a rope or chain which, through some reason or another, had become detached. As a rope runner, one usually went in front of the load of tubs to make sure the road was clear. Immediately, it would become clear in the difference in the speed of the tubs behind him and he would dive for the nearest manhole and pray, (I'm speaking from my own experience), that none of the tubs would become derailed whilst passing his hidey hole. Then, when the runner finally came to a stop, what a mess greeted our eyes: coal scattered all over the place, tubs broken, props knocked out of place, sometimes a roof came in, but amidst it all there was a general sense of relief that no-one had been hurt and surprisingly in very quick time things were straightened up and traffic moving again.

---

by default.
[19] Manhole – a recess made in the side of a tunnel so men could get inside and allow the tubs to go by unhindered, such recesses were spaced every hundred yards or so.
[20] Snap – sandwiches taken for lunchbreak.

Working as a pony driver was a truly terrifying job as well, especially when driving by drifters[21]. On one such occasion, a rope runner – called Henry, if my memory serves me well – was working down 5th North at Mitchell Main and his tubs had become stuck. I was chosen to take my pony down to try and drag them loose. Unfortunately, in this case the rope had become slack when the tubs had stopped and dragged on the ground catching the pin and had dropped off the tubs. So, there was I with my horse running down this incline (not too steep fortunately) in front of a train of twenty or thirty empty tubs, hoping I could keep my feet until I reached the next level. When I did, I yanked the horse into it and the tub kept going straight on, knocking a couple of props out on their way. I managed to unhook the tail chain and free my horse and the tubs were hauled back, giving my horse and myself time to dash away. As we ran, the whole of that section of the roof fell in, raining stone and rubble as we did - a narrow escape, if ever there was one! Yes, but all in a day's work.

Although life was hard working as a pony driver, I daresay life was far worse for the poor creatures we worked with. Once underground the ponies would spend most of their lives there, living in stables down in the mine. They were brought above ground once a year for a two-week period and how they loved to run around in the field during this time above ground. The tail and mane were clipped very short for cleanliness in the unforgiving environment and their coat's trimmed to negate the stifling heat in the pits. They needed to get used to being harnessed and handled, pulling heavy weights, using their heads to open ventilation doors, responding to verbal commands and, of course, britching[22].

So, passed the first of my working years, day after days in the innards of the earth at Mitchell main Colliery, running about half naked, beaded with sweat and painted with cuts and bruises. But, amid all the hazards, I was glad to be at work, earning a living and supporting my family.

Talking of hazards, when I look back and recall the appalling risks we used to take I shudder even now, but of course there were good times to remember, like summer mornings walking along the canal bank at five o'clock in the morning, either going to work on the day shift or coming off the night shift. Listening to the birds and hearing the noise of the fish dancing across the water's surface, sometimes even catching a glimpse of them making their incredible leaps into the air. Nature was completely unspoiled, and there were not too many folks to share it with at such a time in the morning. Afternoon shifts were good as well; setting off to work much earlier than needed so one could loiter along the canal bank and make the most of the fresh air and daylight before getting our lamps and venturing underground for what would soon feel like an eternity. It is always important to look for the bright gifts' life has to offer even in what may seem to be the bleakest of places.

One of these brighter moments in life was my bicycle. I had managed to scrape enough money together to buy a second-hand bike for not much money. It was a true Godsend. Now, I could cycle to work, which made a nice change from walking, especially when considering I would have to walk anything up to four and a half miles before even reaching the pit face. One day, cycling to work along the canal bank and not really taking much notice of what I was doing, I rode straight into the canal. A chap who was walking

---

[21] Drifters – men who were drilling and blasting their way through rock and stone on a new coal face.
[22] Britching – turning around in a small, confined space.

by the canal helped me out. Fortunately, I had spent many an hours swimming in canals before and had no issues getting myself out, the issue was retrieving my bicycle. I asked for his help in retrieving it from the swampy canal, 'Nay lad,' he said, 'Leave it and get yersen home,'. When I told him, I need my bicycle to get to work, he was much more readily available to help me. Imagine that? Fishing for a bicycle in the canal.

After a time at Mitchell Main Colliery, I moved to Houghton Main, a five-mile journey from home. Fortunately, I wasn't expected to walk it but instead travelled in a paddy[23], and what rough rides we had to endure, especially when the driver had been delayed by one or two late comers and had to make up for the lost time so we could get to the pit on time. Even worse, on foggy mornings, one of us men would have to volunteer to sit on the running board in order to give the driver directions in the bad weather.

At Houghton, I worked in both Melton Field seam and the Barnsley Bed seam, and my job was pony driving as at Mitchell's. After a year or two of working with ponies, I had become adept at handling them, although there were still the more fractious types that would cause a real headache. One such pony was Bouncer. The lad who usually drove him was off work on this occasion, so I was asked to drive him. He had a nasty habit of kicking out whenever he felt the weight of the timber after detaching it from the tub and one had to keep a firm grip on his rein with one hand while lifting the timber from the tubs with the other. This was a much better strategy as it meant Bouncer's hindquarters were always away from you, as to avoid a good kicking.

Surprisingly, I'd managed quite well with Bouncer for all the shift. It was on the way back to the stables, travelling along the airway through haze of dust kicked up by the men and horses travelling in front when it happened. I'd turned back momentarily to steady Mike, the pony behind me who was almost treading on my heels, and as I turned back forwards, wham! I felt a stunning blow and saw a great light flash in front of me. Bouncer had stopped, kicked out and I had turned around right in time to catch to blow on my jaw.

I was told later by the ambulance man at the pit head that I was very lucky that the blow had only been a glancing one, otherwise it probably would have broken my neck. That night, I had a very rough night's sleep, with a headache and toothache, pain of which, even in all these years, I have never felt anything compared to it. Nevertheless, I was back at work after three days and I was back driving Bouncer once more.

Because of issues like this with temperamental horses, we were not allowed to ride the ponies but, of course, we did. I do recall being caught once and I was fined half a crown[24]. It doesn't sound much now, but in the days when a packet of ten cigarettes was two pence, it was a fair amount of money. Back then, there were two hundred and forty pence in a pound, so although two pence was not much at all, I still couldn't afford to buy cigarettes, much less pay fines for riding ponies!

Now, when ponies couldn't be used to move tubs – mostly when the incline was too steep for the pony to hold back on its own – we had another method. We pony drivers, on approaching the incline used to insert lockers between the spokes of the back wheel of the tub as this would stop the wheel from turning and acted as a brake for the horses. The lockers were made of wood and metal. I preferred the wooden ones: they

---

[23] Paddy – a thirty-ton Chevrolet lorry with forms placed down each side of the back and protected from the weather by a canvas cover.
[24] Half a crown – twelve and a half pence in modern day currency.

had a piece of wood about a foot long and tapered at each end for entry in between the spokes and the thick part in the middle prevented the locker going right through. The metal ones were made out of iron, again about a foot long and an inch thick, with handles at one end to facilitate handling them. Usually at the approach to the incline there was a supply of lockers and room for the driver to stand and insert them as the tubs went by. It was quite a tricky job and it wasn't unusual for the driver to miss them, then it was a case of hoping for the best, though expecting the worst.

After this brief spell as a pony driver at Houghton Main, I managed to get a job at Barnsley Main which was only 10 minutes' walk from home and also happened to be were my brother, Willie worked, in fact it was through him I got the job. I had applied unsuccessfully on two or three occasions, so I asked our Nip to go in the office with me. He said to the Under Manager 'Can you find my brother a job?', the reply was quick and positive and that was it, I was on the payroll and started working up 93's Jinny. This was what we called a self-acting incline, far more innovative than the colliers at Mitchell Main or Houghton, with an endless steel rope running around a huge pulley at the bottom. At the top there was a brake attached to the pulley and a man was stationed there to operate the same on receiving appropriate signals on the bell.

These inclines were called self-acting because the weight of the full tubs travelling down pulled up the empties, one had to be sure not to get too many empties on it or the rope would come to a stop without the aid of a brake. Of course, the tubs travelling down were held by a chain at the back and sometimes if one of these sets of four tubs became derailed then the chain would continue and cause a bit of a pile up and I tell you these pile ups took a fair bit of sorting out.

It was my time as a pony driver at Barnsley Main where I suffered one of my worst injuries down in the pits. It was at 93's Jinny, near the end of the afternoon shift and I was pulling some empties up. Having gone as far possible with the chain on the front of the tubs the chain was taken off and the hook was attached to the top of one of the tubs further back, then with three or four laps of the chain round the top, one held the other of the chain to keep the laps tight and pulled so taking the empties a few yards further. Unfortunately, as I walked along, pulling the chain, I stumbled and my free hand grabbed at the other rope which at the time unfortunately again, was passing through a small pulley so I ended up with three fingers of my left hand being crushed.

When the Deputy was attending to them, the Colliers on their way out were passing remarks such as, 'Never mind Harold tha's got some more fingers on t'other hand,', very helpful I must say. Anyway, I made my way out of the pit and set off to the doctors whose surgery was on the way home. When I got there his wife told me he was at the club, so I retraced my steps back to the Conservative Club to fetch him. When we got back to the surgery he undid my bandages, took one look and said 'I can't do much to them tonight' bandaged them up again, asked me if I smoked and when I said yes, he gave me a handful of Egyptian cigarettes and asked me to pay him a visit in the morning.

What a painful night I had in store for me; I didn't bother going to bed. Our Willie, my elder brother stayed up with me and I might say those cigarettes were very much appreciated, in the end that little accident cost me seven weeks off work and I still have the scars to remind me.

Later on, I managed to get a job in the main plain, the road which takes full tubs into the pit bottom and brings the empties out. My job was referred to as 'lashing on'; I attached the chain to the tubs and then to the ropes. To do this, one would have to take the chain in one hand with enough slackness to throw four laps over the rope with the other hand. It was a tricky job, especially whilst the rope was running and one rarely had time to stop it unless it was absolutely necessary, as the minute traffic stopped the phone was ringing and someone of authority was demanding to know what the trouble was. Doing this, it was important to be careful of the fingers, but as I have said before, one got used to the necessary risks and in no time, I became quite adept at it.

As I have mentioned, my family was very poor and during this time in England's history, it seemed the country was struggling economically, especially for us poorer households. In May 1926, there was a general strike which brought the whole country to a standstill and had mining areas like Barnsley on its knees. At only fourteen, I didn't really know much about it, but I remember there were men everywhere: miners, dockers, shipbuilders. It was, of course, a time of great worry for everybody, as money was in short supply without the men working, even with Unions helping families with money and food. In our house, money was always a worry, so our financial troubles and strife's were nothing new.

I hadn't been working long at Barnsley Main when my younger siblings started work as well as Willie and me. In those days, the girls went into service, working for rich people by washing and cleaning. In 1928, my sister Linda started working for my Dad's sister Aunt Harriet and her husband George in Leeds. They loved having her, and actually wanted to adopt her, but Dad said that he didn't have so many children that he was starting to give them away. Then, in 1930, my sister Ann went into service in Leeds, and my brother Harry started work soon after in 1932.

It was a good job they'd all found work with such ease, especially considering what was to come. In 1932, having reached the age of twenty-one, I was a top rate employee which was no good for my employers when they could employ younger lads on haulage jobs for half the price. I found myself unemployed along with three million others, so the next twelve months were spent signing on three times a week at the Barnsley Labour Exchange. And the days I wasn't collecting my dole, I was racing my bike to different pits in the area trying to get another job. As most Under Managers came from the pit around the same time, it was difficult to see more than two in one day, not that it made much difference as it was always a fruitless effort.

What the family call my Al Capone photo.
This was the height of fashion.

Our Nip (Willie)   Me aged 21.

Ann

They say the Devil finds work for idle hands to do, but in my case, it was during this period of my unemployment I became converted and joined forces with the *Salvation Army*. And there begins another story, and the beginning of my new, very different life.

It happened in Birstall, while I was on a weekend visit to see some relatives. Spontaneously, I had gone to the *Salvation Army* Sunday evening meeting. Why? I'm not quite sure, but I'm glad I did, experiencing the penitent form and finding God.

On returning home to Stairfoot, I joined forces with the local Corps[25] and it was there I met a girl who, in five short years would become my wife and mother to my children, Lieutenant Daisy Richardson.

The next few months were quite different to anything I had experienced before in life and I found myself saying and doing things that I never dreamed of in my wildest imaginations. Taking part in Open Air[26] Meetings, singing duets with Willie, testifying, knocking on doors, collecting and inviting people to attend our meetings. What a far cry it was from the mucky mines and mile-long walks lit only by oil lanterns! There was quite a few of us young chaps all out of work and the Captain and her Lieutenant were wise in finding jobs to keep us occupied and out of mischief as, previous to conversion, we would have spent our time playing cards and enjoying other gambling games. Cigarettes and alcohol were out when I joined the *Salvation Army*, and although I wasn't much of a drinker, I did enjoy a smoke. I put my packet of cigarettes on the shelf at home and left them there, and I have never smoked a cigarette since.

Still, between our meetings and Godly work, we would make our thrice weekly visit to Barnsley, joining the queues to sign on and draw out our dole. After six months, it was all stopped, and we were forced to take a means test. Introduced by the government in 1931 to reduce costs, officials would evaluate whether an individual was entitled to monetary support by visiting their homes. If you owned anything, you had to sell it or you didn't get any money. It was beyond degrading, so much so that I do not care to dwell on it, even in writing this.

This time, now dubbed by historians as the Depression, was when work was in very short supply and we unemployed were forced to join huge queues outside the labour exchange and wait hours, just to reach the front of the queue and sign a register proving you were unable to work.

Sometimes, when luck was on my side, I could find work in Leeds. My Uncle George Barron, where Linda was working and lived with, had a brush factory, making brushes from coconut husks. During the depression, I would often work for him, labouring and generally helping out. Otherwise, I spent my time making daily trips to the pits in search of a job.

'Hope deferred maketh the heart sick.'

I tell you I learnt the truth of that proverb in those days and so did many other of my fellow workers. These circumstances continued for about twelve months until I was

---

[25] Corps – *Salvation Army* terminology for a group where they worship.
[26] Open Air – a meeting held by Salvationists in the open street.

fortunate to get a job again at Mitchell's Main, as a pony driver. I could hardly believe my ears when I was told to start at the night shift, driving. Why, I thought, what a funny little gift, I used to do this job when I was fourteen years old, now I'm twenty-one, but what a shock awaited me.

Mitchell's Main had changed in the years since I'd last been down there. The roads were so bad, with dirt piled high in between the rails, low roofs and tunnels so narrow that the tubs could hardly get through. Indeed, conditions were so bad that the Corporal (a chap I knew from my early days and who was accidentally killed some time after I left) was with me each time I went into the face with the empties and brought out the full tubs. We arranged a situation for these dangerous circumstances: if I was in front of the load he stayed behind, for if the back tub came off the rails I couldn't get by to attend to it, likewise if the front tub came off the rails he couldn't get by from the conditions being as I described earlier. This happened very frequently, not much of a doddle, eh?

It was here, at Mitchell's Main that I showed my colours as a Salvationist. One night whilst in the face attaching a load of full tubs one of the men asked, *'Harold, do you go to the Sally Army?',* on asking the reason for his question he said it was because I never swore. How funny. From that moment on, most of the men respected my commitment and dedication to the Army.

Later on, I was transferred on to the haulage in the main plain, by this time clamps were in use, which was far safer than what I had been accustomed to. It was during this time I had written to the *Salvation Army* authorities, asking permission to court Lieutenant Richardson, as per *Salvation Army* regulations at the time. Since then, this regulation has now been rescinded but at the time this was necessary, as she was a *Salvation Army* Officer. *Salvation Army* regulations stated that an officer can only marry another officer or resign from Officer ship. I was but a soldier; but I had felt the call to be an Officer and had made the necessary application. In the meantime, life went on at the pit and in the Corps and we were very happy. Daisy was full of life and fun and a rare spirit, something which was to stand her in good stead during the twenty-five years or so in later life when she would find herself confined to a wheelchair, but I will come to that later...

As I said, life progressed at work and we were keeping busy at the Corps, the hall was filled at most of the meetings, so much so that broken seats and makeshift chairs were brought forth and Willie, I repaired them. Life was happy enough, although I did often worry a lot especially about my job. Daisy was a big help to me. I remember she bought me a Poker Work Motto[27] to hang in my bedroom. The words were *'Don't stain today's blue skies with tomorrow's clouds'*, good advice even now, which I tried to follow, but down the years have often failed.

Around this time, I was transferred to another part of the pit, to 3rd North at Billingley the district where, as I mentioned earlier, I used to pony drive for the chaps who were driving through the coal seam. Well, in the years I had been away at the other pits, a new coal seam had been found and now was in full production so I was kept busy lashing on the full tubs that were on the way to the pit bottom and the empty ones to be taken into the workings to be filled. It was rough, dirty and often dangerous work, but I

---

[27] Poker Work Motto – text burnt into wood with a poker.

was happy to be working, knowing that I had some saving to do in order to get to the *Salvation Army* Training College.

Not long after this, in July 1934 whilst I was working nights. I came home from work one morning to find Mum had delivered a baby child, her eleventh child. The 'midwife' – I must use this term lightly as she was just another neighbour who was used to helping out during these situations – had said there was another babe on the way. No antenatal care then, and Mum hadn't realised she was having twins! We spent a restless day worrying as we feared for Mum's life and the life of the unborn child. It was with a heavy heart that I went back to work that night, and to say it dragged slowly would be an understatement for I was wrought with worry.

After work I hurried home, dreading the news that I might receive on my arrival. When I got home all was well, the second baby was born just before midnight and Mum and the baby, a boy, were both okay. With the birth of Daisy and Dennis, who just managed to have birthdays on the same day, the family of Sam and Ethel was complete. With seven sisters and four brothers, our family had finished growing – the twelve Cloughs.

The following months seemed to pass quite uneventfully. I was quite happy at the Corps and at work. Then, as if things seemed to be going too smoothly, I received another jolt in January 1935. I had an appointment with the Candidates[28] Secretary regarding my application for Officership and, would you believe it, that very same week I was given a weeks' notice to leave my employment. Of course, there were many others besides me, but under the circumstances that knowledge didn't help much. I was accepted for Officership and received into the next session of Cadets[29] due to enter the *Salvation Army* Training College the following August.

Although I tried my best to get a job during the next few months, it was to no avail, so it really was a struggle to get the necessary outfit together in time for the August session. However, with help from the comrades at the Corps and generous friends and neighbours, obstacles were overcome, and I left home in August 1935 to enter the Training College at Denmark Hill in London. Apart from occasional visits to nearby relations this was my first ever departure from home, so I approached it with some trepidation. A poor mining lad from Stairfoot in London, who'd have thought it! How I wish I could go back and tell my Headteacher about this.

London! What an eye opener to one who had previously never travelled any further than Barnsley and its neighbouring towns. The traffic, the busy railway terminals and the prospect of underground travel were especially fascinating to me, though the part I liked best was the riverside, the Old Father Thames of the song. Any opportunity – and I must say these were to be rare during the next few months – I grasped to stroll down by the river, though in later years as a family we visited London fairly frequently so there were more opportunities of sight-seeing in the future with my girls.

College days, what can I say? It was a time of really intensive study and practical training; almost every minute of the day was planned out, from waking up in the morning at seven o'clock to closing your eyes at ten o'clock, just in time for lights out. For the next ten months (apart from a few days of Christmas leave, which I must say were very welcome) the time was spent learning, Bible Study, Field Training[30] and visitation.

---

[28] Candidate – a term used in the *Salvation Army* for someone who has applied to be an Officer and is waiting to attend the training college.

[29] Cadet – a person attending the training college.

Monday afternoons, from lunch to seven o'clock was scheduled free time and while most Cadets went to see the sights, I (being rather short of money) used to take a tram to Victoria for two pence, and then a bus to Fulham for three pence to call on Daisy's family. It was a bit awkward on the first occasion having to introduce myself, as they had only heard of me in letters from Daisy; but after the first visit and the initial strangeness I was always very welcome and appreciated it very much.

Daisy's family were quite different to mine. She was the youngest of a family of four brothers and two sisters. In childhood, she'd had a younger sister named Winifred, but in those days, it wasn't unheard of for children to die young. She had died from infantile paralysis at only five years old; this was an illness probably similar to modern day polio. Daisy was the youngest by five years to her nearest sibling Stanley. Her family were quite fortunate financially, with her father always being in work as a hansom cab[31] driver. In fact, he was the first person to drive a motor driven one in England, instead of the horse drawn ones of the time. Later, as times changed, he became a taxi driver. They were probably quite worried about me, as I'm sure they were not happy when she told them she was planning to marry an out of work miner.

Thinking about it, they were quite a bit better off than my family. They were probably quite worried about me when she wrote in her letters about courting and intending to marry someone they had never met and who was out of work! Of course, circumstances meant the Richardson's could afford a better life. With the age gaps between children, all except one of Daisy's older siblings were married, so there were only three people living there. It meant there was a lot more room in the house and a lot more money and food to go around! To me, her house was a palace, with an extra bedroom, and they had a garden and their very own toilet at the end of the garden – a far cry away from the 'luxuries' of Albion Road.

The difference in our backgrounds was highlighted at the beginning of my Christmas holiday from College. For some reason Daisy had decided she would call at my home to collect my suit. Of course, in our home, anything not being worn was at the pawn shop, and that was exactly where my suit was. When she told me about her visit, we had our first big row. I told her she had no business turning up at my home uninvited, not because I was angry but out of embarrassment that she should discover how poor we were. In no time, we soon made up and forgot about it. Daisy wasn't actually bothered about us having to pawn things, it was just something that didn't happen in her family.

Life continued on much the same for me in London. Studying, occasionally visiting Daisy's family in Fulham and again, more studying. Though, I do recall a rather interesting event I was able to see whilst at college. In January 1936, King George V died, and I went to see him lying in state at Westminster. What crowds! It was unbelievable to someone not used to such things – for me, a miner's boy who played on slag heaps and was left in awe at the grandeur of having your own tippler toilet, to be paying his respects to our late King.

As I recall my college days, it reminds me of all the extraordinary things I was able to see and do. It seems I did most of my travelling with the *Salvation Army*. In the November of my college days, I was sent to Scotland with the Cadets to campaign across the country in groups of about ten. My group went to Coatbridge in Scotland and we had quite a rousing

[30] Field Training – learning how to conduct meetings, this was practiced at the Corps adjoining the College which was, in my case, Battersea and Wandsworth (a Young People's Training Corps) and Westminster.
[31] Hanson cab – a horse-drawn carriage.

time and enjoyed it very much. Later on, during Self-Denial[32] Period, we Cadets were sent to various Corps to assist with the collecting. I was sent to Clacton-on-Seas and then, at Easter, I was with a group sent to Tunbridge Wells.

All in all, college was a very enlightening time in every sense of the word; but I couldn't mix as much as I would have liked as I had to be careful with what little money I had. Most of the other chaps seemed to have lots of money to enjoy their free time with and most took the opportunity to visit the expensive sights in their free time which, unfortunately, I just couldn't afford to do.

It was in 1936 that my family would leave their home in Barnsley for Keighley, a mill town in West Yorkshire. It was primarily so the girls would be able to find work as there was not much going for them in Barnsley as a mining area. Keighley, on the other hand, had a lot of textile mills employing women. Linda stayed in Leeds with Aunt Harriet and Uncle George and I, at the end of my Officer's training course would not be moving with the family but waiting to see where I would be sent to continue my work with the *Salvation Army*.

Eventually, commissioning day[33] arrived and what excitement I felt, feverishly preparing for the big occasion at the Royal Albert Hall and wondering where I would be appointed. In my case, it would be Denby Dale.

Denby Dale, like Keighley, was in West Yorkshire, situated about halfway between Huddersfield and Barnsley. My Captain was a chap named Alf Mitchell, about my own age. Despite our many differences (which is only natural with two different personalities), we got on rather well together and had a happy time at the Corps.

It was here that I learnt to play the cornet[34]; the bandmaster, Herbert Noble was most helpful in the endeavor. Still, I wonder how he didn't get tired of me asking what the different notes were, especially in the middle of open-air meetings though I'm sure he'd be pleased to know his teaching did not go in vain – I didn't stop playing until I was ninety-seven! At ninety-seven I was the oldest bandsman in the United Kingdom, imagine that, who'd have thought it? And I was still playing Solo Cornet until that age in *Silsden Town Band* which I joined in about 2004. I also became quite good at playing the concertina[35] not long after learning the cornet, learning to play on Daisy's when I became an Officer. A few of us formed a concertina band and we cycled around areas for a few days holding a campaign with open air meetings trying to give out the Christian message.

As Lieutenant and second in command, I spent a lot of time with the young people's side of the Corps work and was responsible for distributing the *Salvation Army* papers across Denby Dale. With these jobs, my bicycle became very useful once more for keeping in touch with the surrounding villages. In my spare time it meant I could cycle into the countryside which I found very enjoyable as Yorkshire has some beautiful dales to admire.

---

[32] Self-denial – this was a period in the *Salvation Army* calendar when people were asked to deny themselves so that they could give money to the poor, in this country and abroad. As well as asking Salvationists to give money, the Salvationists collect from members of the public in what is termed door to door collecting. This, as the term suggests, is knocking on each door in an area.

[33] Commissioning day - the day the cadets were appointed as Salvation Army Officers.

[34] Cornet – a brass musical instrument.

[35] Concertina – a musical instrument, played by holding in both hands and pulling and closing the bellows. The sound is made by free vibrating reeds on metal.

During this time, Daisy was stationed at Worsborough Corps, about twelve miles away from Denby Dale. My own Captain was quite sympathetically inclined to our relationship, he himself being engaged, and was quite generous in giving me some free time to go courting whilst I passed my first year as a *Salvation Army* Officer. The people of the Corps at Denby Dales were very helpful to me in my first year; I think they seemed to favour the young Lieutenant who seemed to get just about all the sympathy that was going!

It was while I was stationed at Denby Dale that the abdication of King Edward VIII took place. I remember quite well all the speculation and the uproar when the news broke about the affair with Mrs Simpson.

After twelve months at Denby Dale, Captain Mitchell and I were transferred to Hillsborough, a Corps in Sheffield and I stayed there until the November of that year when I moved to Langold, a small Corps near Worksop. This was the first Corps I was in charge of myself. What an eye opener it was at Worksop! My domesticated youth came in handy when I had to give the place a good scrub in order to make it somewhat presentable to invite people into; it was dirty indeed. However, a few of the soldiers rallied around and, despite a few difficulties, we didn't do too badly in the few months I was there. I got on quite well with the people of Worksop, especially with it being a mining district and I having been a miner myself.

My next move was to Bircotes, another mining village a few miles from Langold. It too was a small Corps with very few soldiers, but they were very warmhearted and helpful; though it was here that I found the quarters[36] none too clean, in fact the Divisional Commander[37], organised some helpers from nearby Doncaster to come and help me give it a good scrubology[38], as I was feeling a bit fed up, what with a dirty hall at my first Corps and dirty quarters at my second. However, the blessing of being able to serve the people far outweighed the setbacks and I must say I learned that a sense of humour was a great help both in those early days and in later days of my Officership. Years later in the 1960's, musicals became very popular in the *Salvation Army*, just like the secular musicals but with a religious message. A song in one of these was *'Cleanliness is next to Godliness'*, when I heard it my mind went back to the dirty halls and quarters I had been sent to. Some things you never forget!

It was at Bircotes that I received a lot of help from a young man called Claud – his mother and the others of the family were very kind to me, and I was welcome any time to have a meal with them. Claud worked in the nearby colliery of Harworth, but on the outbreak of war in 1939 he joined up, I heard that he had reached the rank of Sergeant, but he later was killed in the Middle East. Such a tragedy, but I was blessed to be an Officer in the *Salvation Army* and have the wonderful opportunity of meeting these colourful people I would never have had the chance to know otherwise.

From Bircotes I was transferred to Buxton in Derbyshire and moved there on the week before Christmas 1938. There was an eventide home[39] run by the *Salvation Army* at Buxton and I used to conduct meetings quite regularly for the old people who usually

---

[36] Quarters – a house provided by the *Salvation Army* for their officers to live in.
[37] Divisional Commander – officer in charge of an area which contained several corps. This person did not look after a corps.
[38] Scrubology – a term used when a group of people meet together to clean a building. It is a term and indeed a practice still used in Churches and *Salvation Army* Citadels today.
[39] Eventine home – home for the elderly.

appreciated the time spent with them. The Officers in charge of the home were very kind and I was always welcome to have a meal with them too, this was very much appreciated and made a nice change from preparing one's own meals.

Being a young man myself, I always paid attention to the youths and tried to organise things for the teenagers in the evening. I forget which Corps I was at at the time, but on this particular occasion a group of the boys were causing trouble and I had to turn them out of the Youth Club. Once they had gone, everything went smoothly, and I thought no more about the incident. That is, I didn't until I had locked the hall up and was walking home. It was a dark night and I suddenly became aware of footsteps following me, unfortunately it wasn't simply the footsteps of one or two people but many more. Undaunted, or rather trying to appear that way, I continued walking home. It was of course the youths I had turned away earlier. They continued following me and then came the menacing chant, *'Rush him, rush him'*. I don't mind admitting I was scared, but continued on my walk home, eventually reaching my door. I unlocked and opened it with trepidation expecting to be attacked at any second, but I walked through the door, locking it behind me, all in safety. The threat was over!

Another troubling incident occurred at the Corps when the coal man couldn't get to the boiler room and he had tipped all the coal in the passage outside the hall. I was shoveling the coal to move it to the boiler room, feeling very much like the young boy I was years before, dancing on slag heaps for dosses of coal to sell, when a chap passed. Stopping, he said to me *'I'll come to your meeting, you're the first one of your lot I've sin wi tha coat off working in ya shirt sleeves'*. Even now, I am humbled by this, I have always prided myself on being an honest working man.

I remember that winter was quite severe with plenty of snow and, because of this, Self-Denial was particularly arduous, especially with such few soldiers to help with it. On Friday evenings I used to go pub booming[40] in the surrounding villages in Derbyshire. Two particular villages stand out in my memory Doveholes and Birdsedge, both quite isolated and, for a few weeks, the snow was piled at the sides of the roads, so travelling was quite difficult especially in the dark. However, on the arrival of spring, what a difference, such lovely countryside which was most enjoyable to cycle around during pastoral visits and on Corps business.

It was during my time in Derbyshire that the date of my wedding was becoming ever closer. I was very much looking forward to July 1st, 1939, to marry my beloved Daisy. In the late spring of 1939, I was moved to Eckington in Derbyshire and, during the next few weeks, between getting to know the people and finding my feet with the usual Corps duties, I spent the time preparing the quarters for my wife, and believe me, although it was only a matter of weeks, to me it seemed ages until July 1st.

The wedding was to take place at Daisy's home in London, so on June 28th I set off for Fulham. On arrival I found Daisy ill in bed. A clothes prop had fallen and knocked her on the head, causing an abscess to form over her temple, it was so bad that she was taken into Fulham Hospital in the early hours of June 30th, so naturally there was some confusion regarding the wedding arrangements. We prevailed on the doctors to allow Daisy out of the hospital for the wedding and reception on the understanding that she returned to the hospital that same evening, and that is exactly what happened. So, in 1939 Daisy and I were married on the 1st of July, we became Mr and Mrs G. H. Clough, –

---

40 Pub booming – selling *Salvation Army* publications to public house customers.

this turned out to be not long before the start of World War Two, only two months later on the 1st of September 1939.

The medical staff were not very happy about Daisy leaving hospital, but she was a determined woman and was adamant that the wedding would go ahead. There were relatives travelling from Yorkshire and Scotland, and she wasn't prepared to let them spend their hard-earned cash for nothing. Maybe she'd learnt a thing or two from my northern ways?

The next week was supposed to be our honeymoon, but it was spent on the hospital ward, holding hands during visiting hours and around doctors prodding and poking at poor Daisy. Fortunately, the next week we were able to travel to Herne Bay, a seaside town in Kent. Originally, we had booked to rendezvous in Ramsgate but under the prevailing circumstances we had to cancel, though our holiday to Herne Bay was most enjoyable. We had a lovely time, though Daisy had to endure some painful sessions having her wound dressed, but we were fortunate enough that our landlady, who had been a nurse, was happy enough to do what was necessary. After our week in Kent, we stayed in London for a week and then returned to Eckinton to take up our Officership duties.

In the early days of our marriage, before children came along, we would spend much of our leisure time with Daisy's brother, Stan and his wife, Grace. Like us, Stan had also trained to be a *Salvation Army* Officer and had attended college the same year as Daisy, so we all had a lot in common. It will sound strange to you all now, but Daisy often used to laugh at the fact she was the only woman in her session at college who was able to mix with a man. During those days, the training college was fiercely segregated by sex but as brother and sister, Daisy and Stan were in college together, they were fortunate enough to be allowed the same free time to visit home together.

I recall one such occasion when Daisy, Grace, Stan and I took an outing to the seaside. Daisy's sister, Ivy and her friend were usually with us on these trips as well. We would wear the silliest of swimming costumes, though they were very fashionable at the time, and the ladies always wore swimming hats covering their hair. On one of these outings I managed to get sunstroke and sunburnt, the only time I've ever suffered with either to date! It was a glorious day and we enjoyed it playing around in the sea. Afterwards, we came out of the water and had our picnic, not bothering to get dried and dressed as it was so warm. This was a big mistake in my case as I realised later that evening. My skin was bright red, I felt to be on fire, and I was extremely sore all over, I felt as if I had been beaten, added to that I had a terrible headache and felt sickly. Obviously, I had spent too much time in the sun. This was a lesson well learned and I have never sat around in the sun for very long since that day.

Of course, our life was not all seaside's and holidaying as you can well imagine. And, in the earliest months of our marriage, Daisy spent much of it in terrible pain. The next few months were quite an ordeal for Daisy as she suddenly lost the use of her hands and her fingers. Apparently, some of the poison from the abscess had found its way into her nervous system and affected the use of her arms and hands. I had to do her hair, tie her shoelaces and many other little things she no longer felt capable or confident enough to do.

During this time, she was a regular visitor to the doctors to have injections in her arms which we prayed would encourage some improvement. Those in themselves were quite painful and left her arms sore and aching. We traipsed from hospital to hospital, visiting Sheffield on quite a few occasions but little improved, which left Daisy a little depressed and we both began to wonder if there was going to be any improvement. She lost her sense of touch and couldn't write, however I tried to help her as much as I could. Fortunately, her usual cheerful disposition and unbounded faith brought us through and gradually she began to improve and was able to do things again, which after so many months was a great relief to us both.

Although this was a happy little win in our family of two, it seemed things would not be so bright for much longer, with the approach of the Nazi threat and the looming prospect of war hanging over our shoulders. It seemed much harder times were destined to come.

Salvation Army Citadel in South Yorkshire.
Unfortunately I can't remember which corps it is.

I'm on the second row, third Cadet from the left. This is the group of Cadets from the Liberator Session who were assigned to the Battersea group.

I'm on the second row, second in from the right next to the flag carrier.
Another group of Cadets from the Liberators Session.

WILLIAM BOOTH MEMORIAL TRAINING COLLEGE
THE 'LIBERATORS' SESSION
1935-1936

CADET___George Harold CLOUGH___

APPOINTED AS___Probationary Lieutenant___

TO___DENBY DALE.___South Yorks. Division___

The Salvation Army

WILLIAM BOOTH, FOUNDER   EDWARD J. HIGGINS, GENERAL

NATIONAL HEADQUARTERS

14th May 1936

Whereas _George H. Clough_
was received into Training for Officership
in the Salvation Army,

Now in consideration of
satisfactory reports having been received at the
completion of Training, the said

George H. Clough

is to the Glory of God and for the Salvation
of the people hereby **COMMISSIONED** as a
PROBATIONARY OFFICER of The Salvation Army.

As witness my hand on behalf of the General
of the Salvation Army.

William F. Rich

BRITISH COMMISSIONER

N. 306—1,000

Me as a young Lieutenant.

Daisy and me.

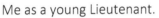

FROM HOSPITAL TO WED—BACK

For four hours a girl was allowed out of hospital on Saturday—to get married.

She was Miss Daisy Richardson, a Salvation Army officer, of Bullow-road, Fulham, who had n in the hospital several days.

ne was married at the Methodist church. ndsworth Bridge-road, and after cutting her dding cake at the reception in the Salvation army Hall, Walham Green, she returned to hospital.

Her husband, Mr. G. Harold Clough, also a Salvation Army officer, from Sheffield, spent Sunday afternoon, which was to have been their honeymoon, at her bedside in the hospital.

Miss Richardson was determined that nothing would inconvenience all her relatives and friends, some of whom had travelled from Scotland not knowing that she was in hospital.

aldine House. Rolls Bldgs., Fetter-lane London.

Our wedding photo was taken in the weeks after the ceremony due to Daisy's illness.

Our honeymoon in Herne Bay.

My Dad, Sam in the normal fashion for working men at that time. If popping down to the pub, he would often put a muffler (scarf) around his neck.

War was declared in September, with the German invasion of Poland. We all knew it was coming, but it didn't mean we were any less surprised. Life for the next few years would be quite different, and even more so in the years beyond the war.

For us, food was in short supply, especially after the government introduced a system of rationing. We were supplied with ration books and only allowed a certain amount of some foods per person. I remember eggs were in very short supply and dried egg powder became the norm for us. Daisy made these into a good meal by mixing it with milk and making 'pancake' eggs, a bit like an omelette. She would also mix mashed potato in sometimes to make it more filling. Mum's recipes of our poverty-stricken childhood were also a good stand by.

Make do and mend became the word to live by. Daisy, being a very good sewer, was excellent at this new way of life. Torn sheets were turned, that is the edges were sewn together, the sheet was cut down the centre where it was becoming worn and then hemmed so this became the edge of the sheet. Clothes were unpicked and new ones made using the wrong side of the material. Knitwear was unpicked and new garments made out of the old wool. Some old sheets and pillowcases were made into petticoats, blouses or shirts. Her mind was impeccable, and her creativity seemed endless, it seemed like a lifetime ago that she was bedbound, unable to move her hands and fingers and she made new creations in the blink of an eye.

In spite of the war, we continue to go to London for our holidays to see our relatives. But we didn't stay very long as we were always conscious that we were taking someone else's place when we used the air raid shelters.

Although it was always a joy to see the family, it was truly frightening spending time so close to the capital. I remember hearing the doodlebugs[41] flying over the city and we, along with so many others, would stop in horror hoping and praying that the engine wouldn't stop as that signified the bomb would fall and devastation would ensue. When we had our eldest daughter, Sylvia in 1942 and took her down to London to meet her family, her hearing must have been very keen as she always heard them approaching before us. Luckily enough, the little tyke wasn't old enough to understand what they were!

As *Salvation Army* Officers, we were both exempt from active service in the armed forces, but we always tried to do our bit to help the members of the services and keep spirits up in our community.

We always wore our *Salvation Army uniforms*, they were our work clothes and people recognized us because of them, knowing we were there to help people in any way we could, big or small. We were travelling by train one day when a member of the Military Police, accompanied by a drunk soldier came up to us to ask if we could do him a favour. His dilemma was clear, the soldier had to return to duty, but the M.P. was worried that in his drunken state he wouldn't be capable of changing trains, which was essential for his journey. He left the soldier in our care and we ensured he caught the correct train, thus ensuring that he finished his leave without a mark on his record, for the only other alternative would have been for the M.P. to have arrested him.

---

[41] Doodlebugs – The Luftwaffe's V-1 flying bomb used against the Allies and dropped throughout south-east England.

We often billeted soldiers, either as they were passing through on their way home, or to their new appointments, or just because for some reason they needed a bed for the night. During those times, people helped because they could, without asking questions or favours in return. A united nation was vital and offering a helping hand to those in need was always the best way to achieve such things in my opinion.

At this time, we were still stationed at Eckington, situated between Sheffield and Chesterfield. It was quite a small Corps and despite Daisy's illness we were quite happy there. When war broke out in September the place became a depot for the R.A.S.C. (Royal Army Service Corps). A lot of soldiers were moved in, and I feel were able to be of some help to quite a few, especially as in the early days of the war the billets for the soldiers were rather overcrowded.

When winter arrived, we had quite a lot of heavy snow. I remember we used to go out to the various places where soldiers were housed and take hot drinks; I believe it was appreciated and I certainly like to think our small acts of kindness encouraged some cheer in those dark, lonely times for the soldiers. We got on very well with the neighbours too and in May 1940 when we received orders to move, they were sorry to see us go. However the *Salvation Army* wheels turned and we were moved to West Auckland, but we didn't stay there very long as conditions were not conducive for Daisy's continued recovery, the main thing being that all our water had to be carried from a tap outside; this among other things made our stay there a very short one.

Due to the difficulties arising from the circumstances with our quarters and Daisy's ill health we decided that we needed to be near our family. It was about 1940, and we took some home leave, and went to Keighley to stay with my Mum and Dad. They took us in and made their front room into our private accommodation – like a modern-day bed-sit, sharing kitchen and bathroom facilities. After a couple of weeks, I managed to get a job with the local *Cooperative Dairy Company*. I delivered milk. The milk float was electric, and I pulled it around the streets to do my delivery. We kept the *Salvation Army* authorities aware of the situation and I recall that they were not at all pleased to hear I was working as I was still employed by them, but we were not being paid by the *Salvation Army* while we were on sick leave and we needed to live and pay our way. I felt it was unreasonable of them to complain as we couldn't expect my parents to continue to pay for our living indefinitely.

After a time of sick leave, Horwich was our next appointment, situated near Bolton in Lancashire. We arrived there in time for Christmas 1940. During this time, cities nearby like Manchester and Liverpool were being heavily bombed, so we could see and hear what was happening, us being only a few miles away. Having such atrocities going on at our doorsteps reminded me of our frightening holidays in London. It was only a few weeks after moving that a land mine was dropped on an estate near to the quarters; fortunately it landed on a patch of soft earth between some houses, which cushioned the blast and though there was quite a lot of superficial damage there were no serious casualties. It did, however, keep me alert to the situation of the War, and I would always count my blessings for having avoided these near misses.

Unsurprisingly, we had heard the noise of the land mine falling and I was getting my shoes on ready to go out and see if I could be of any help to anyone, when one of my soldiers came up to me and asked if I was going out to help with him. I was amazed that he had come straight into my house without his usual habit of knocking, it wasn't until a moment later I realised our front door had been blown off by the blast of the bomb. Imagine that, and neither Daisy nor I had even noticed!

We were prone to these attacks very often. Although Horwich was only a small town in Lancashire with a population of about fifteen thousand at the time, it was nestled in the centre of a triangle of three much larger towns in West Lancashire – Preston, Wigan and Bolton. It also brushed shoulders with various other towns, Blackrod, Farnworth, Kearsley, Little Lever, South Turton and Westhoughton meaning it was a nifty place for the German's to bomb. Unsurprisingly, Horwich was on the Luftwaffe's route to bomb Liverpool and also the home of *Horwich Loco Works* who constructed just short of five hundred tanks during the War, The Cruiser, Mk VIII, Cromwell (A27M), the Centaur (A27L) and Infantry Tank Mark II or as it became known the Matilda II.

In the late 1930's, a shadow de Havilland aeronautical engineering factory was hurriedly built in a farmer's field in Lostock, near Horwich. It was a large windowless shed built as Britain clambered to join the arms race. The shadow factory produced thousands of propellers for the Hurricane Fighters and the iconic Spitfire that played such a significant role in repelling the German's during the Battle of Britain. I recall in early 1940, in a six-week period, the factory had managed to produce over a thousand constant speed conversion kits for the British fighter planes. Such input raised the profile of our small and seemingly insignificant northern backwaters and, unfortunately, Horwich's efforts had not gone unnoticed by our enemies in central Europe. It seemed that 'doing our bit', although it had been a flurry of success, it had also brought greater dangers to our doorsteps.

The Luftwaffe adopted their best practices in their efforts to incapacitate the industrial heartlands of England. Our German enemies would use our geography to their advantage: Rockhaven Castle stood on Winter Hill to the northeast of Horwich and it proudly rose over the countryside and its shadow cast an eerie cloud over the lush green meadowlands, providing the Luftwaffe bombers with the perfect geographical landmark to use to their advantage. Once they had spotted Rockhaven Castle from the sky, it took little effort to find Horwich and its Locomotive Works further south in Lostock.

The Manchester Blitz hit Horwich hard as well. It saw the German Luftwaffe bomb the large city and all its surrounding area, from Sunday 22nd December to Tuesday 24th December. It seemed we were given our Christmas holidays from the bombings! There was just short of seven hundred fatalities and over two and a half thousand people were injured. It had been preceded by what became known as the Christmas Blitz, where Liverpool was targeted on the Friday to the crossover day of Sunday; in effect, the Nazi's had spread their blanket bombing throughout the northwest of England. London was no longer the sole target of those Luftwaffe bombs. Fortunately, the bombing decreased in severity after the New Year. Needless to say, I think Mr. Hitler could have kept his early Christmas presents and left us quite happy and alone.

Talking of this reminds me of a silly rhyme the youths would sing to keep spirits up during these seemingly endless and ruthless bombings:

'Careless talk costs lives.
Mr. Hitler wants to know!
He wants to know the unit's name.
Where it's going – whence it came.
Ships, guns and shells all make him curious.
But silence makes him simply Fuhrious.'

In hindsight, Horwich may seem like a rather dangerous location to you now, but we had some very happy times there as a young couple. Whilst in Horwich, Daisy and I bought ourselves a tandem bicycle[42] and it was very useful to us during the following years as Daisy struggled to ride a bicycle on her own in her condition. We used it often to go pub booming on Friday and Saturday nights to collect from the outlying districts and, on one such occasion, we travelled all the way to Keighley on the tandem – that was quite a journey I can tell you now!

In those days, there were not many cars on the roads. Cars were for the rich people or doctors who needed them for professional purposes, and we fit into neither of those categories. Instead, we relied on our tandem for both leisure and work. Thinking of happy memories on that tandem always reminds me of this silly little song I would sing to Daisy, it always made her smile:

'Daisy, Daisy, give me your answer do,
I'm half-crazy all for the love of you,
It won't be a stylish marriage,
I can't afford a carriage,
But you'll look sweet,
Upon a seat,
Of a bicycle made for two'

Being *Salvation Army* Officers, neither Daisy nor I had much of wage. In fact, sometimes if there wasn't enough money for us to be paid our full salary, we simply didn't get it. Our Corps people were working class people and they were poor also, but we always got by. We rode on the tandem, a second hand one that I picked up cheaply, to meetings, band and Songster practices and to visit our Corps folk. It was either ride the bike or walk, we didn't have money for bus fares.

As Officers, we always wore our uniforms as we were always working, regardless of where we were or what we were doing. When riding on the tandem, Daisy's bonnet could sometimes be a little uncomfortable, but she put up with it and kept it on. The bonnet was tied at the side of the head with a big bow and the ribbons were quite long. She told me that when she was in Training College as a Cadet training to be an Officer a friend had gone out on a bike and taken her bonnet off, tying the ribbons over the handlebars. Unfortunately, the ribbon got stuck in the spokes of her front wheel and the lady came off her bike, being thrown over the handlebars and landing on her head, resulting in her death. Thus, Daisy's bonnet stayed firmly on her head. We had some grand times out on that tandem. I remember one day after cycling up a steep incline, Daisy asked if I had found it easier peddling. Thinking about it I realised that yes it had been easier for some reason. *'Good!'* the reply came back quickly and with a cheeky smirk, *'I was actually peddling for once'*. We had many a laugh about that incident.

We spent a very happy nine or ten months at Horwich, but as it always goes with the *Salvation Army*, our time had come to move on. Though the Corps was very small, with only one or two comrades in uniform; I like to think we were of some little help to

---

[42] Tandem bicycle – a bicycle with two seats, one behind the other so that two can ride the same bicycle.

them during our stay. In fact, one comrade and I kept in touch and exchanged the occasional letter until her death a few years ago.

Soon, we found ourselves stationed at Lamberhead Green where our first daughter was born. We called her Sylvia. As it was March, and we were still at work, I spent hours and hours collecting on my own for Self-Denial as Daisy couldn't work and what soldiers we did have were busy helping with the war effort. Sylvia was born in Billings hospital in Wigan and so we had ourselves a Lancashire lass!

Daisy was only tiny and had quite a bad labour, but both her and Sylvia were okay fortunately. Sylvia was a healthy baby, but we did have a worrying time regarding her health on a couple of occasions. She was only a few months old when, one day, Daisy went to see to her, and she had some kind of fit and didn't appear to be breathing. Daisy grabbed hold of her in a panic and ran for help. The doctor said that Daisy's quick thinking had saved her life and she had no ill effects, fortunately. The next time was when she had measles. She was really poorly, and we sat up with her for three consecutive nights praying for a smooth and quick recovery. We were worried because she didn't seem to be able to hear. I asked Daisy during the third night if she would like some tea and toast. How thrilled we were to hear a little voice pipe up with *'I want some tea and toast'*. In those days there was no National Health Service and we had to pay the doctor. Most doctors paid someone to collect their money and it was usual to pay an amount of money each week for this. Although we struggled to scrape the money together to pay for Sylvia's healthcare, it was always worth the struggle to see her happy and healthy again.

Our next move was to Blackburn Fishergate, it was there that I conducted five funerals of old folk belonging to the Corps. Again, it was quite hard work there being so few workers, and in order to be able to collect and visit it meant we had to leave Sylvia in the care of different people which really wasn't fair to her. We did not stay here long, moving to Blackburn and then to Barnoldswick. From here, it was fairly easy to cycle to Keighley to visit my family. Of course, the tandem wasn't any use to us now as we had a youngster, so unless we were visiting for a few days I would go by myself for a few hours. My sister Kathleen was now old enough to cycle back with me sometimes, to spend a few days visiting us and then I would ride back with her.

Not long after this, some of Daisy's family came to live in the north. Although northern cities were receiving their fair share of bombing, it was incomparable to the horrors going on down in London, as we always saw on our holidays to visit Daisy's parents. Unsurprisingly, Daisy was becoming quite worried about her family, what with all the children being evacuated. Even Norman, Daisy's young nephew had been sent away, but had become very ill in his short stay of evacuation and was sent home to recuperate.

On hearing about this, my dear old Mum had insisted that my wife's sister Mary and her son come to Yorkshire to stay with them. Mary and my Mum became great pals, and Norman thrived in the Yorkshire air and had a great time going to school and joining in the fun and games with my younger siblings and their friends. They both stayed there safely until the end of the war. I can't remember the sleeping arrangements, but Mum always coped somehow. My parents were never wealthy as you well know, but what they lacked in money, they always made up for with their great big hearts! Thinking of it, I think Mum was happy to have the company, they used to go to the local pictures together and became good friends. If I remember correctly, she was still with my Mum and Dad when my father died shortly before the end of the war in February 1945 from an asthma attack. He had always suffered from asthma and his work as a coal miner in Barnsley and latterly his work in the textile industry in Keighley would not have helped the condition.

It was very nice to live so close to both lots of families, and although the war was still raging, we felt much less scared at the threat across the pond, now that we were surrounded by our loving family.

My brother Harry in his uniform during the War. I can't remember what he did during the was, but he was stationed in Iceland for a time.

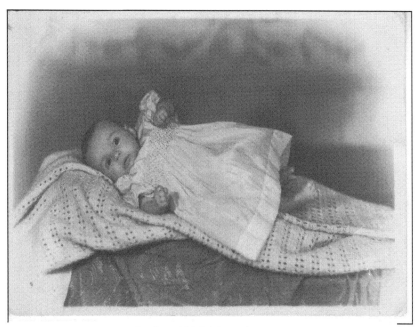

Our first child, Sylvia was born.

My sister, Mary, on her wedding day to Norman Boothroyd towards the end of the War. I remember there was difficulty with the registration of their marriage as Mary's middle name Elizabeth hadn't been registered, this had to be rectified a few days later.

5| New Horizons

In the summer of 1945 as the war was nearing its end, while stationed at Barnoldswick, my wife and I decided that we would call it a day and resign our Officership in the *Salvation Army*. We had devoted a lot of our time to their efforts, but it was time to put away our uniforms and spend some quality time with our families. So, in August 1945 we left Officership and moved to Keighley, we thought we would settle in Keighley because that's where my family lived.

We initially moved in with Mum and my brothers and sisters who were still at home. Ann, her husband Ernest and their son Peter were using the front room, so we were given the attic for our families use and Mum and the older girls slept in the front bedroom whilst the others used the back. Considering the number of people living in the house things ran very smoothly. Although my family was large, we had all always got on well together.

Obviously, this situation wasn't ideal for anybody and when Charlie Nicholl's offered us a lease on the basement in the shop we leapt at the offer. It was certainly no palace, but we were happy to have the space. Being a basement, it was quite dark and dismal, but it was our new home. As Officers we had always lived in furnished accommodation owned by 'the Army' so it was like starting all over again. We found ourselves searching to find some furniture for ourselves quickly. Money was in short supply so we sold some of the wedding presents that we could manage without to get things we needed for our home. The basement was a Godsend for us, but there were still difficulties as one can imagine. One was that the only entrance was by a flight of about ten steps, and Daisy was pregnant, so using a pram would be difficult. The other snag was that the toilet was outside, up the stairs and across the yard. Not ideal but it was our home.

The baby was due in November 1945, our second child, but Mavis put in an early appearance, arriving in the October. She was to complete our family of four. She turned out to be quite an active child, a climber if you will and I daresay she could probably climb as soon as she could walk. She was always getting up to mischief and discussing this reminds me of one such incident in 1946 when she was less than a year old. Daisy had left the children in the basement while she had gone across the yard to the lavatory. Upon her return, she found Sylvia, who was about five at this time, standing in front of the bookcase with her arms out and Mavis, about four foot off the ground, sitting on top of the radio. Our little monkey had managed to climb up three shelves of the bookcase and on top of the radio!

In 1945, all in all, life was good. I had a job working at *Widdops*, a marine engineering company which made engines for ships. Initially I was a labourer, but I soon progressed to driving overhead cranes until I eventually became a Radial Driller. I enjoyed my work there very much as it was most interesting and I felt proud of the hard work I contributed, especially when I saw one of the engine loaded on the wagon ready to transport, knowing a lot of the work put into making it had been done on my machine. We also had our own little home below Nicholl's Radio Shop, which proved to be beneficial for us. Charlie as well as selling radios, Charlie mended them too, often having to go to people's houses to do this, so he had to close the shop. Once Daisy knew this, she told him to give her a shout when he was going out and she would listen for customers coming into the shop so that he didn't have to close and risk losing business.

By this time, we'd also settled nicely into a routine and had settled well into our local *Salvation Army* as soldiers. I used my musical skills on the cornet to play in the Salvation Army band and would often play on my concertina to accompany singing in the meetings when the band wasn't playing.

During this time, I also taught myself how to play the mouth organ, deriving a great deal of pleasure when I was able to play a great deal of tunes once I had heard them once or twice. When the children were little, although money was still tight, Daisy bought me a present of a chromatic harmonica. What pleasure I had from this over the years. Unlike my other instruments, which proved useful in providing music for meetings, I played this just for my own satisfaction and enjoyment. Daisy wasn't musical but she had a piano accordion, so I learned to play that too, but it wasn't really an instrument I was comfortable with as I found it rather bulky and cumbersome.

Having always enjoyed singing, it was during this time I joined the songsters[43] and Daisy attended the Home League[44]. Daisy didn't join any musical groups as she was no singer and wasn't too keen on brass bands like I was, but she always encouraged me to take part in these sections and was always supportive in attending meetings and concerts I played in. We always managed to keep ourselves busy. Before long, Sylvia would be starting at Holycroft School.

After the war the government ran a scheme encouraging men to train to become teachers. The six-year war had caused a rift in education, after huge numbers of men who would have gone into further education after school (either to university, teacher training college or some other kind of training) had gone to war instead. Because of this, teachers were in short supply and Daisy wanted me to put myself forward to train as a teacher. We discussed this and I was not keen on the idea, we had a young family and I didn't feel that we could afford for me not to be working so I didn't pursue this. I've never regretted this as I have always been happy in my work and enjoyed working, always being grateful that I have been in employment and we were able to pay our way.

We settled down well in Keighley. For a time, we were worried about Mavis as she was slow to talk. There was a radio programme at the time, where people had difficulty understanding someone and the catch phrase was 'What's Horace Saying?'. This soon became our cry to Sylvia as she always knew what Mavis wanted. My mum would always put us at ease and said Mavis was simply a lazy baby and didn't need to speak as she always got what she wanted without. Eventually, she began to talk, and life continued very well. The firm I worked for was always busy and although we were no longer Officers in the *Salvation Army*, we had linked up with the Corps in Keighley and, to a large extent our lives revolved around this.

We were still leasing the basement flat but had our names down with the council for a house when one was available. The council had a huge building programme going on after the war, building prefabricated bungalows at Woodhouse and Bracken Bank, made out of steel and prefabricated concrete. Although we liked our makeshift home under the radio shop on South Street, it was no longer an ideal family home, especially with the heavy winter snow we had been dealing with. I well remember the winter of 1947,

---

[43] Songsters – A choir.
[44] Home League – Ladies meetings.

morning after morning having to dig my way out of the basement and making a path across the yard to the toilet; it seemed to go on for weeks. The winter was the worst of the century and the public acclimatised to the difficulties of the war, soldiered on.

Within no time, our lease was up on the basement flat and we still hadn't got a house, so we returned to Mum's attic. Charlie was a good friend and actually offered to lend us the money for a house, all drawn up legally at the same rates as banks would charge, but we felt that it was too much money to borrow and decided against it. Perhaps a missed opportunity but again not one that I've regretted. Then, one day in March 1947, my wife proudly walked into our home in the attic dangling some keys, a look of sheer joy on her radiant face. We had become the fortunate tenants of a brand-new council house. So, you can imagine our delight the day Daisy came dancing into the house with a bunch of keys telling all and Sundry that we had a house!

When we got the house, there was only two and a half rows of the new houses and about half a dozen stone-built terrace houses above these. At the front of the houses was farmland, and an underground reservoir and at the back it was grassland. This was later built upon and it became the Bracken Bank Estate. There were so few houses that of course there wasn't a bus route and we had to walk about a mile to the nearest bus stop which was Ingrow.

We moved in at the first opportunity and my sisters, Ann, Ada and Mary were kind to offer to help us clean the house up. In no time, it was spick and span and oh, what a luxurious home we found ourselves in! We had three bedrooms, two of them were double bedrooms with radiators and the third was a single bedroom. We had a bathroom with a bath, wash hand basin and toilet, a huge hall with storage under the stairs, a big kitchen with four floor-to-ceiling cupboards and a stainless steel sink and draining board with space underneath, which Daisy covered with a curtain, and attached to this was a work surface with two cupboards underneath. And a gas oven. We had a dining room with a radiator and a big sitting room. There was a fire in the centre of the room which was fuelled by coke[45] – this heated the radiators and the water. What bliss after the rooms we had been living in!

Added to this, we had a porch outside the back door, and an outside toilet off the porch and a large coal house where I would be able to keep my bike and garden tools when I bought some, for we had a big garden at the back and the front of the house. Our land was initially just soil and rock and rubble but the potential for gardens was there. We couldn't believe how fortunate we were. I can't say I ever really enjoyed gardening and, to be honest, it was often a chore, but we had a large back garden and a decent sized front garden with our council house. Once I had cleared the ground at the back, I grew vegetables which helped feed us and my Mother's household, eking out the housekeeping. In later years I made this into a lawn with a rockery garden and path in the front of the window. Although I had very little free time and wasn't keen on this work, I must admit to being quite proud of my front garden, which although I say it myself, was always one of the best on the street.

Life continued on much as it had before, and Sunday's remained especially busy for our little family of four! In the morning, Daisy would stay with Mavis while she was a baby and Sylvia and I would go to the Citadel[46]. I would leave Sylvia in Sunday School,

---

[45] Coke – a derivative of coal, a process removes all the gas from the coal. It is a smokeless fuel.
[46] Citadel – the hall where our *Salvation Army* services were held.

while I went to the Open-Air Meetings, then, afterwards, Sylvia would join me for the following meeting. In the afternoon we all went; Daisy taking both children to Sunday School while I went to the Open-Air Meeting, then we all stayed for the meeting afterwards. Home for tea, then we all went back for the evening Open-Air Meeting in the Town Hall Square, followed by the evening meeting, followed by a prayer meeting and then a Wind Up[47]. This set the pattern for Sundays for many years. Daisy used to stay home in the mornings to make the dinner but as Mavis got older, she also attended morning Sunday School and when they were old enough the girls would sometimes go home on the bus instead of going to the morning meeting. By this time my sisters' children also went to Sunday School so there were enough of them to be sure they would all be safe. When the girls were old enough, we got them bikes and they used to cycle to the Army with me.

During this time, I took leadership of the Songsters, a job I loved, as music had always played a big part in my life and I love singing. Before this I had been the Corps Sergeant Major, a role where I was responsible for giving the announcements in meetings and making sure things ran smoothly. Daisy was a Sunday School teacher and a member of the Home League. Unsurprisingly, she was always in high demand as a speaker at Ladies Meetings at other Churches. She also spent a lot of her time visiting the Corps members who had fallen ill. It seemed, once an Officer, always a dedicated Salvationist!

Not long afterwards, Sylvia decided she wanted to join the Young Peoples Band at the *Salvation Army*. Girls weren't actually allowed to join, but with the same determined spirit as her mother, she was adamant that she wanted to learn to play the trombone. She already played the piano, so didn't need to learn to read music, she wanted to know the shifts, or whereabouts she moved the slide to get the notes. She was soon proficient and ready to join the band. She joined along with her friend Barbara. This was a milestone, girls in the band. Some years later, I taught Mavis to play the baritone when she was about twelve years old. Both of my daughters have continued to play throughout their lives, and I feel very proud when I listen to them playing.

Although my bicycle was handy to ride to the Army, I always rode my bike to work. It was especially helpful when I worked overtime on Tuesday and Thursday evenings. These were long days as I went straight to Songster practice from work on Tuesdays and to band practice on Thursday evenings, but it was always worth it as I loved to sing and make music! I often worked on Saturday mornings too. In fact, when I first started, Saturday morning was part of the normal working week.

I returned home from band practice one Thursday, to find the house in uproar. Daisy had been making cocoa for the children at bedtime and, to ensure there was no accidents, she pushed the cups to the very back of the work surface as the drinks were hot. Mavis had tried to get her drink and, of course, the hot cocoa went all over her arm. There were no telephones in those days and Daisy was at home on her own with two children, Sylvia about eight years old and Mavis was only four. As soon as I got in and saw the situation, I dashed straight away and ran to the doctor's house. I explained the situation and the doctor said he would come straight away. I walked the mile back and quite soon Doctor Robert attended and cleaned and dressed her arm. Daisy had to take her to the doctor's surgery each day for her arm to be cleaned, swabbed with penicillin

---

[47] Wind Up - another meeting of singing, testimonies and pieces played by the band and songs from the songsters.

solution and clean dressings applied. Thanks to this and the discovery of penicillin the burns healed quickly and without a scar.

Thank God for the National Health Service, all this was free! Even then, money wasn't plentiful, but we got by and Daisy was a good manager. She bought material from the market and made clothes for herself and the girls and she always knitted cardigans and jumpers for all of us. As I mentioned earlier, I watched my Father mending shoes and using his Last and tools I tried my hand at Cobbling in the hopes of saving some money. I continued to do this for my family for many years, also mending the shoes for my Mum and my brothers and sisters.

Mondays were always wash days, so on Sunday nights the wash tub, a galvanised steel tub, was brought from the coal house and filled with hot water to which washing powder was added. The clothes were added and the posser[48] put in the tub and used to agitate the clothes. It was a rule that anybody going into the kitchen for anything would have a few turns of possing the clothes.

On the Monday morning when I had gone to work, and the children were at school Daisy would start doing the washing. Before I went to work, I moved the washtub nearer the sink and added more warm water and brought the mangle in from the coal house. Daisy would wash the clothes using a block of green household soap on dirty parts and then rub these on the washboard[49].

To dry, the clothes would be put through the mangle to get the water out of them. The water from the tub was emptied and then refilled with clean cold water and the clothes were popped back into the tub to be rinsed. The clothes were then put through the mangle again, then folded and put through again so as much water was squeezed out of them as possible. It was a time-consuming job and hard work. To wring the clothes the wet clothes were held in the left hand and fed into the rollers of the mangle while using your right hand to turn the handle which worked the rollers. It wasn't easy to do and could be dangerous as my sister Mary found to her cost. Whilst feeding the clothes into the roller she got her hand caught, to release her hand she had to rewind the roller, thus crushing her hand twice. It was a nasty accident and her hand was swollen and bruised for weeks, but fortunately she suffered no lasting damage.

I remember we used to use *Dolly Blue* to whiten the clothes, it was some sort of powdery stuff in a muslin bag. After the washing, of course, everything had to be dried and we would hope for a dry day so that this could be done by hanging them on the clothesline outside. If it was wet everything had to be dried on the clothes horse round the fire which seemed to take ages.

In the 1950s we upgraded our washing facilities and bought a washing machine. This was an electric machine consisting of a tub and a mangle but not as hard work although the same procedure had to be gone through to rinse the clothes, but the water was agitated by the machine and the mangle was worked by electricity. We upgraded again in the 1960s to what was known as a twin tub. What luxury it was with its tub for washing the clothes, attached to a spinning machine which was done all by itself! To rinse the clothes in the spinner, a rubber tube was fitted to the cold water tap and the water was piped into the spinning machine on top of the clothes. The lid was closed, and the water was spun out of the clothes via a tube at the bottom of the machine, which was

---

[48] Posser – a copper bell shaped implement with holes in which was fitted on a wooden pole.
[49] Washboard – a corrugated piece of galvanised steel set into a wood frame for ease of holding.

placed in the sink, so the water drained away. If it was still soapy more water was added to rinse the clothes.

Later on, I bought an Automatic Washing Machine of the type that most people use today – what luxury and what a speedy, easy procedure: just putting the dirty clothes into the machine, selecting the type of wash required and pressing a button.

The girls and I always came home for dinner and as wash day was a hectic day, there wasn't much time to cook a meal, so Monday dinners were always cold meat from Sunday's roast and Bubble and Squeak made with left over vegetables from Sunday. Delicious served with pickles or sauce and bread and butter. The roast was made to go a long way and on Tuesdays, some of it would be minced and cooked with onions for a tasty meal with vegetables and if there was any left on Wednesday this would be made into a hotpot. We didn't have fridges in those days, just a pantry for keeping food cool, but it seemed to work alright, because the meat always lasted, and we were never ill.

Other times, we didn't have leftovers but enjoyed some lovely treats. One night a week we would listen for the Pie and Pea Van. Sylvia and Mavis would go down the snicket onto the next street with a large baking bowl for pie, peas and mint sauce for four. A Fish and Chip Van would also come around one evening a week. They were delicious treats indeed and made a nice change from leftovers.

I remember coming home one morning and Daisy telling me she had got a job working mornings at the *National Switch Factory* based at Ingrow. She told me my sister Ann would look after the children until it was time for them to go to school and that as her work finished at dinner time, she would meet them and take them home for dinner. Both girls were pupils at Ingrow County Council School. I was furious! I was from the era where women did not go to work, they stayed at home and looked after the house and children. Her working caused quite a few arguments and I was glad when she eventually left work and life returned to normal.

In the 1950s, Daisy started having problems with her hands again, she would sometimes drop things and would suffer terrible pins and needles or, even worse, the feelings in her hands wasn't there at all! I also noticed that she was dragging her leg. She obviously sought medical advice and had various tests and was eventually diagnosed with Cerebral Neuritis, the only medication they offered were vitamins, as they said there was no treatment, no cure.

By this time, Daisy was the Corps Cadet Guardian[50] at the *Salvation Army* and as her walking deteriorated, it was more difficult for her to use the buses to attend the group as there was quite a walk from the bus stop and I was usually out at Songster practice. How kind our neighbours were, as one of them would wait for her and help her home. Although life could be hard sometime, we managed to struggle through, with the help of our family and the kindness of our neighbours and friends.

Shopping also became rather difficult, but we had always had the bulk of our groceries delivered, but of course there were some things needed from the town. Our next door neighbour was brilliant and always did our shopping with hers. The girls who went to Grammar School by now, would also call at the shops on their way home from school.

Around about this time, as Daisy's condition worsened, was the Coronation of Queen Elizabeth II. This was being televised – not of much interest to us as televisions

---

[50] Corps Cadet Guardian - the leader of a Bible study group for teenagers.

were not widely owned and we certainly didn't have one. However, our neighbours and friends Mr. & Mrs. Reece bought one especially for the occasion and invited us all in to watch the ceremony. How exciting this was! The house was full of people and we all had a brilliant day and were enthralled by the little box in the corner, bringing us pictures live from London. She looked so young to be Queen.

We got a television set in 1955. One or two of the neighbours had them and Daisy was sick to death of Mavis wanting to go into someone's house to watch their television and she worried that she was being a nuisance. Charlie's Radio shop had expanded to become Nicholl's Radio and Television Store, so Daisy discussed renting a television with Charlie. Yes, I did say renting! Televisions were expensive and people didn't buy them. Charlie told her that the Purchase Agreement had to be signed by the man of the house. This wasn't going to happen Daisy told him, there was no way that I would agree to it, and she intended to have a television. So, Charlie agreed to let Daisy sign the forms and the set was delivered to our house. Programmes were all in black and white, no colour television for quite some time, and they would start with children's programmes at teatime, adult programmes started later into the evening and it all closed down with an epilogue before midnight.

It was in this same year of 1955 that a young lady, who had been in my wife's Sunday School class came to live with us as her parents were moving to Huddersfield and she didn't want to go. She had a job in Keighley and lots of friends mainly going to Keighley *Salvation Army*. Joan soon became a part of our family, she was seventeen when she came to live with us and lived with us for four years, leaving when she got married and moved to Grimsby. We have remained friends all these years. When Daisy was in a wheelchair, we spent many happy holidays with Joan and her husband Leonard at Grimsby and nearby Cleethorpes, where I was able to push the chair on the promenade and round the shops as the area was not hilly like Keighley. We went there for many years and had lovely holidays, our last one being just a few weeks before my wife's death.

During this time, people started to travel a lot more. Many people enjoyed holidays abroad in the late 1950s and early 1960s, but we were happy with what we knew. Prior to holidays abroad, Holiday Camps had been quite popular with some families or stopping at the seaside at Guest Houses. People would travel to these on public transport – the bus or the train.

Our holidays were always spent in London, so that Daisy could see her Mum and the rest of her family. She travelled on Wednesday before the feast holiday with the girls and I would travel down on the Friday night. The mode of travel was steam train. To ensure that the girls had a proper holiday, we would always see the sights in London, like proper tourists, something I couldn't afford to do when I lived there in the 1930s as an Officer in training. We saved all year to afford the holiday, but it was always worth it to see the delight on the girls faces as they sat on the fountains at Trafalgar or river boated down the Thames. One incident with Mavis was while we were on one of these holidays in London and thinking about it still brings a smile to my face. We went for a boat ride on the river Thames, she was only a toddler and she took her shoes and socks off as she wanted to paddle. I had a dickens of a job keeping hold of her. It's amazing how strong toddlers are. In that moment, I vowed that I would teach both of my girls to swim (I was always aware of the episode where I cycled into the canal and could have had a far different outcome if I hadn't been a good swimmer!) as I wasn't sure how much longer I could hold onto dear little Mavis before she divebombed straight into the river!

It was after one of our lovely holidays, in the late 1950s when we had a major problem. *Widdops,* the engineering firm I worked for was moving to Scotland! The government was trying to increase work in Scotland because work wasn't plentiful and were offering firms incentives to move there – *Widdops* decided to take up the offer. We were devastated; our lives were running smoothly and now I was going to be out of work. Clifford Shuttleworth, a friend from the *Salvation Army* told me to go to *Prince Smith and Stells*, a large engineering firm in the town, and I got a job there. It was a huge firm, and I had been working in a much smaller set up at *Widdops*, I hated it! Fortunately, I only needed to stay a few days, because *Metal Box Company* based at Shipley, offered me a job that I had applied for, so I left and started work in Shipley.

I settled well there and liked the work, but one day I had a visit from Jim Whittaker, an old colleague from *Widdops*. He had set up his own engineering company and he offered me a job. I started working for him at *Sealand Engineering* and stayed there until I retired at the age of sixty-five. Initially, the firm was in the Ingrow area, but he later moved to Oakworth, both places near enough for me to cycle – although the hill up to Oakworth was a little harder to tackle – but I cycled to work until retirement.

Although I spent a lot of time at work, and we were heavily involved in the *Salvation Army*, we were a very close little family and spent many hours together doing things as a family. We used to play board games – ludo, draughts, snakes and ladders, as well as numerous card games – rummy, sevens, twist, snap, pairs and patience; and tiddly winks was another favourite game. We enjoyed many a happy time as a family together, in between our busy schedules.

From left to right back, Ada, Mary, Harry, Annie Bernard. From left to right front, Daisy, me, Mum, Kathleen and Linda. Dad had already died, and Willie did not join the family in the move to Keighley, instead staying in Barnsley.

From left to right, Willie, Me, Bernard, Harry and Dennis. The five Clough boys.

Left to right, Mary, Ann, Kathleen is standing behind Ann, Ada, Daisy, Annie then Linda who is seated. The seven Clough girls.

Daisy and I with Sylvia, proud parents.

Young Mavis and Sylvia.

Daisy and I with Sylvia and Mavis at Trafalgar Square, holidaying in London.

In my garden at Bracken Bank. I lived there for fifty-one years.

Me with Tessie, the Winter of 1976.

Me with Daisy, Sylvia and Mavis.

6| Father to Grandfather

During the 1960's, the girls left home to get married and start their own families. Our family extended to include three grandchildren, Nigel, Sharon and Mark. Sylvia and Mavis used to come home to help around the house, but my sister Ada lived a few doors away from us and she popped in to check on Daisy several times a day. This was good because it enabled me to keep working.

Daisy's illness had progressed, and she was now only able to go out in a wheelchair. She pottered about the house with great difficulty and tremendous will power. She had several falls, which were actually her illness getting worse and after each fall her mobility decreased. As the disease worsened, we were eventually able to get a *Home Help* to clean the house.

Despite this we were able to have outings with our daughters and their children and spent many happy hours at Bridlington, Morecambe, Blackpool and a particular favourite place was Burnsall, where we would picnic, and the children would play around in the river.

We also continued to holiday in London with Daisy's family. After her Mother's death in around 1958 her sister Ivy and her husband Dick would also travel to Yorkshire to spend holidays with us. I had always got on well with Daisy's family and Ivy and I were great pals. Her husband was a marvelous help with Daisy when we were with them. Nothing was too much trouble for him.

I had never been one for going on trips organised by work, as I found that the men liked to spend a lot of the time during the day drinking and then again they liked to stop at the pub on the way home, being a non-drinker I found this quite boring and preferred not to go.

However, in the summer of 1977 Jim Whitaker was organising a work's outing with a difference; it was to the launching of a ship in Sunderland on the River Wear as *Sealand*, the company I worked for, manufactured components for the shipping industry. My son-in-law, Edgar was working with me at that time during his holiday from Teacher Training College, and he had been invited on this day out, so we both decided it would be a good day. The ship was built by Austin Pickersgill who produced a successful range of SD14 ships which contained many *Sealand* engineering parts. We travelled to Sunderland by coach and arrived at the yard to see many hundreds of people waiting there. The launch of the ship itself was a very exciting experience with all the dignitaries and work people present. The ship was named (I wish I could remember what it was called) and the usual bottle of champagne was smashed on its bow. At the same time the wedges holding the ship were knocked away. The ship then slid slowly at first into the narrow river before creating large waves as it hit the water at speed. The ship was then restrained by large chains which stopped it crashing into the opposite bank. The large waves continued to reverberate for some time along the riverbanks. The newly launched ship would then have to be fitted out ready for delivery to its new owner. The whole experience for us landlubbers was well worth the visit to see the birth of a new ship and I considered myself very fortunate to be part of that experience. However, the day wasn't over yet, because arrangements had been made for us to have a meal at a restaurant in Ripon, which was very nice. After the meal, Edgar and I took the opportunity to look round Ripon Cathedral which finished off the outing really well.

I became good friends with my sons-in-law and Edgar and I often went on walks together. Sometimes the boys came along and other times, it was just the two of us. I had always enjoyed walking and loved these days out, seeing the countryside around where we lived.

I had always kept an eye on the football results regarding Barnsley, but Sylvia and Robert took me to watch Huddersfield Town play. I became quite a fan of that team. I thoroughly enjoyed these outings on Saturday afternoons though I did miss Daisy and felt bad at leaving her at home, but when the stadium became all seating I stopped going. I felt the atmosphere had changed and it wasn't as enjoyable. I've always taken an interest in the team since then and was overjoyed to see them promoted to the Premiership in my one hundred and fifth year!

I retired from work when I was sixty-five years old, after fifty-one years of work. I loved work from the day I started in the mine until the day I retired, and always thanked God that I had a job to go to and that I was fit enough to do the job. If circumstances had been different, I would have liked to work longer but it seemed more sensible to finish work and be available at home for Daisy. It was a very strange week and a very odd feeling indeed, not having to get up and cycle to work. I also missed my dinner time walks around the village of Oakworth and the people I worked with.

On the Saturday of that week, there was a special meeting at the *Salvation Army* Citadel, and I had been asked to sing a solo. To my surprise Daisy said she would like to go too, so Edgar borrowed Sylvia's car and came to pick us both up. It took quite a bit of time to get Daisy in and out of the car and I was worried that we would be late. Sure, enough when we arrived there wasn't anybody about and the curtains were drawn in the entrance foyer, screening the hall from view. Edgar opened the door and I pushed Daisy into the hall. To my surprise there was a loud chorus of *'Happy Birthday!'* and I was amazed to see the hall full of my family and friends. At this point, Captain Melvyn Ackroyd came up to me with a red book in hand and he said to me *'George Harold Clough, This is Your Life'*. Unbeknown to me, my daughters had been contacting people for weeks, asking them to come along on the evening or send greetings to be added to my *'This is Your Life Book'*. It was just like the television programme. The whole evening was centered around me and they had arranged for people to take part in the evening with solo items and recitations. What a wonderful birthday party this was and aged sixty-five it was the first one that had ever been arranged for me!

Our finances changed when I retired as I had no wage coming in. I had always worked but unlike today, not many people had a works pension, so our finances were reduced to the old age pension paid by the state.

For the last twenty years or so of her life Daisy was confined to our home owing to Multiple Sclerosis which gradually got worse, this diagnosis replaced the earlier one of Cerebral Neuritis. However, on the whole she was mostly cheerful about things and wasn't one to grumble about her lot. As I've mentioned, as Daisy's health and mobility deteriorated, I had to help her more. For a long time, getting her upstairs had been difficult and if she had a cold or the likes, this would affect her legs and it could take her half an hour to get upstairs with me having to lift each foot on to each step and then of course it was hard getting her down again the next morning. We were grateful that we were fortunate, and the house had an outside toilet for during the day.

Eventually we decided that it made more sense to stay downstairs and for many years she slept in a very comfortable chair bed in the dining room. I had to help her dress and do her hair and most other things for her. How we laughed when a neighbour who we were great friends with, who had had a stroke, used to come over every morning for me to fasten her shoes. All this before I cycled to work! She must have thought I hadn't enough to do. For myself, I was profoundly glad that I was well enough to look after Daisy until her passing.

At the back with me is Sylvia and Ralph. Seated at the front, Dick (Ivy's husband), Ivy and Dick (Daisy's brother). Holiday time in London. This is taken in Dick and Ivy's garden.

Captain Melvyn Ackroyd presenting me with 'The Red Book' on my sixty-fifth birthday.

Me with my grandchildren, Nigel, Mark and Sharon.

Holidaying in Northumberland with Mavis, Edgar, Nigel, Mark and Sharon. Ralph took the photo.

Daisy died on 19th July 1983. We had been married for forty-four years. Her loss meant I have spent many, many years on my own, and it started a new phase in my life. One of the hardest things I have ever had to do, and the hardest part was finding something to do with all the time I had. For years I had rushed everywhere so that Daisy wasn't on her own for too long, but now there was nothing to hurry for.

Cooking wasn't a problem for I'd been doing that for years, and if I do say so myself, I was quite good at it. As well as cooking dinners, I enjoyed baking and was a dab hand at making pastry. There was never a crumb left on the plate when I made my speciality jam pasty! However, the household finances were a different matter as Daisy had always sorted these from the day we were wed, but there was nothing else for it but to get used to it.

Eventually, I got used to doing all of these things and living my life alone. I began to take my time and stop worrying about doing tasks quickly such as the shopping, sometimes even popping into the café for a snack.

Life continued on rather differently but still, I spent a lot of time at the *Salvation Army*. There were nowhere near as many meetings as there were in my younger days, but I still had the Band and Songsters and Sundays were still very busy. Although I did get used to my new regime and attended functions with other family members, it was never quite the same for I no longer had that special person to spend time with.

The Army still took up a lot of my time, especially over certain periods, such as Christmas and the Self-Denial period. At Christmastime, over the years, I have spent many hours playing carols in the various nursing homes in the area and in the town centre raising money for the Army to give food parcels, gifts and Christmas Dinners to those who couldn't afford things. I was fortunate and privileged to be able to participate in this until the age of ninety-two. I also went door to door collecting for the *Salvation Army's* Self-Denial appeal way into my nineties.

I had many interesting times with the *Salvation Army* band over the years, playing in various meetings or concerts, but I will tell you about the times I was on the television. The first one was at Christmastime and we had been asked to be filmed while we were caroling in Haworth. We took our stand and the television cameras rolled, then they asked us to play it again, and again, and again. All in all, we played 'Hark the Herald Angels Sing' a total of thirty-two times. It seemed the hard work paid off as we were all thrilled to see ourselves on the television for their advertisements of Christmas programmes. Norah, who was collecting for us on the day, was the star of the show. The other time was when we were asked to play in the grounds of Skipton Castle for the Gloria Honeyford Sunday morning programme 'Sunday'. It was the middle of July, but it was a very cold day. We arrived as requested at half past seven in the morning and were given the programme jingle to practice as they wanted us to introduce the programme, as well as play a hymn tune at the end. Throughout the morning other people who were being interviewed or taking part arrived, and it was imperative that we were very quiet as the microphones pick up even the slightest noise. The television personalities being interviewed were Paul Shane and Ruth Madoc from 'Hi-de-hi!'. They were very nice and went out of their way to speak to us all. One of our members Peter Findlay, had us all chuckling when he was telling Paul Shane jokes. The programme commenced at about ten o'clock and ended at about midday after a church service. It was a long morning, but we enjoyed it and it was a new experience. I just wish it hadn't been quite so cold. Of course, we all recorded the programme and watched it when we got home. It was very exciting.

My daughters also attended the *Salvation Army* and we – Sylvia, Mavis, Edgar and I - would often play in the band together and we did so for years. Although Sylvia wasn't playing in the band at the time, she often came along to help us, and it wasn't long before she had joined us on a permanent basis again. At concerts the five of us (my sister Daisy also played) would often perform together, playing marches on our instruments or singing as a quintet, and what happy times we had.

Throughout my life, I have been able to make good use of my musical and singing skills, often being asked to sing solos with Sylvia accompanying me on the piano. I would also recite poems and monologues; I think the last monologue I performed was at a programme with *Silsden Town Band* when I was about ninety-five years old.

In many regards, my daughters were very good in taking care of me and occupying my new spare time in many different ways. Sylvia would take me to football matches in Huddersfield as a keen Terriers fan. I still recall the last match I saw on 27th December 1983, Huddersfield against Manchester City at Leeds Road in the old second division. Manchester City had recently been relegated and were vying to make a return to the topflight, whilst Huddersfield had won promotion in the preceding season. Manchester were in fourth place just outside of the promotion places and Huddersfield were flying high in sixth, not quite a top of the table shoot-out but definitely a promotion six pointer. Manchester City supporters filled both ends of the ground, we were packed in like sardines in a tin. Football now is not like how it was in the old days, football is all about money, it's a business and I have no time for it anymore.

Sylvia, Barry and I would also enjoy watching cricket on Saturday afternoons. Sylvia was a 'scorer' for the local league and Barry was an umpire. I would go along with them most weeks and look after their dog. I spent many happy hours watching the cricket and in between taking the dog for a walk.

Sylvia and her husband Barry would also have their dinner at my house during the week and I looked after their dog while they were at work. This was a Godsend for me because it gave me a purpose in life and also made sure that I was eating. I often used to take Tess, the dog into town with me when I did a bit of shopping. On this particular day I had walked into town, stopping to buy something from the chemist on my way down. Tess was very obedient and stayed outside the chemist, because I told her to. I carried on walking into town and finished my bills and shopping then decided to go to the library. It was only as I arrived at the library, I remembered Tess – I had left her outside the shop. I was quite worried and turned back and, like the good dog she was, she was sat waiting for me just as I had left her. Talking of this, reminds me of another rather humorous shopping occasion, when I had been into town to do my shopping, stopping at one or two of my sisters houses for a morning coffee and then returning home on the bus. As I was walking from the bus stop, I was joined by an old lady who lived on my street, who was bemoaning the fact that she had forgotten to buy something she needed. I said I would leave my shopping at home and would go back into town to get her what she needed, and that's exactly what I did, discovering sometime later than she was in fact ten years younger than me!

Mavis also found good use of my time. For many years, when the blackberries were in season, I would spend hours on the moors picking the fruit and the girls would make them into jam which they sold to make money for the Salvation Army (between us we must have made a fair bit of money for the Army). I would also pick bilberries they were on the bushes, a much harder and longer job as they were much smaller and harder to pick, but they were worth it for the delicious pies Mavis made with them. And, as bilberry pies were Mark, my youngest grandsons favourite, she was always encouraging me to scout for them. With this in mind, I was thankful for the invention of home freezers as we had pies for weeks. Often, they found themselves with too many berries after I had gotten carried away collecting so many and so, the girls still made jams with any leftovers.

I would also spend a lot of time with Ralph, Daisy's nephew. He would often come up to stay with us for a few days holidays and this continued after Daisy died. We would go for long walks together often joined by Edgar. Mavis' husband. On one of his visits, we decided to go to Barnsley. It was years since I'd been back for anything other than funerals. How good it felt to be revisiting the steps of my childhood and youth, and I felt very pleased that I was still able to find my way around and enjoyed showing Ralph around. What great memories that day brought back and how I enjoyed it.

Another visit to Barnsley was in 1984 during the Miners' Strike. Although Nip had passed away years before, his family were still Miners in that area, and I felt it was only appropriate to go and help out as best as I could. The television news was full of the strike and the battles with miners and police. It seemed to be all that was on the television at that time. The accounts of the problems at Grimethorpe were dreadful and I was worried about Willie's family. The strike went on and on and although the mining community pulled together to help each other, they were having a bad time. There were often collections in Keighley and most towns to raise money to help the miners.

Charity begins at home or so the saying goes, so we raised money from family and friends and collected food and toiletries, and whatever people wanted to donate, and Mavis, Edgar, Mark and I had a trip to Barnsley to help our family. They were thrilled to see us and thankful for the gifts which would be shared with other striking families.

This was a time of great sadness for me. I remembered the times my Dad, Nip and I had been out of work and the hardship we had encountered, and here it was all happening again. Whole areas were run down and decimated, shops were closed because nobody had any money to spend in them. The sad part was that the industry never recovered from this and pit after pit was closed, until eventually mining in Britain was no more!

Although this visit filled me with sadness because of the circumstances it was good to meet up with 'our nips' family. It was also interesting to discuss the mining industry with them and the changes that had occurred since my days down the pit. Lots of good changes came about after the war when the industry was nationalised, particularly with the introduction of more safety regulations. Another great change was the fact that the workers were now able to shower before they left work and were clean when returning home. What a great difference that would have made to our family in the 1920's. I was interested to learn also that pit ponies were still used in some pits, but these were few and far between now.

Mark took a great interest in this visit and went to the area by the mine to draw some of the machinery, which he used for his project for his General Certificate of Education O-level examination. Thinking about it, he was creating a piece of history that would soon be no more.

I had never been a keen traveller, but I found myself travelling all across the country in the 1980s. There was a Fifty-year Reunion of the Liberators Session, this was the session I was in when I trained to be an Officer. I decided I would like to go and meet up with these old friends and colleagues once again. The reunion was held in a beautiful building that the 'Army' owned in Sunbury. I set off in a little trepidation, travelling on my own, but I needn't have worried I had a great time. After the reunion I went to Slough to stay with Joan Bell, a friend from my early days as a soldier in The Salvation Army, before I entered college. What a great couple of days we had reminiscing, and it certainly occupied my time well!

Often, I found myself with little time to spare as my large and loving family were always there by my side to make sure I was never too lonely or felt forgotten about. For many years, I was visited every Wednesday evening by my sisters who would come to my house for a game's night and a nice supper. At one time, darts was the chosen game and we had happy evenings with lots of laughter. Mind you, you should have seen the state of my dining room door, it seemed none of us were quite the dab hand at actually hitting the darts board!

Another favourite game we enjoyed was Scrabble, and we kept score meticulously. I'm sure we all won at some time or another, but that didn't stop the friendly squabbles about whether words were allowed or not! At one time, the Officer in charge at the Army, Lieutenant Alan Young would always come to join in the fun with us. We all missed his ready laugh and sense of humour when he was moved to another Corps.

When my youngest sister Daisy finished full time employment, she and I went out together most weeks. As pensioners, we were the proud owners of free bus passes which meant we could have quite a cheap day out and we would travel to Bradford, Ilkley or Skipton to go shopping. I loved looking round the charity shops and we spent hours trailing from one to another looking at the books and CD's. We would then go for a bit of dinner before catching the bus home again. We had always got on well together despite the difference in our age, or probably because of it, because I think I was like a father figure to her as she was only eleven years old when our Dad died.

On one particular Saturday in early July of 2001, I was a little fed up and so I decided I would go through to Bradford on the bus. I popped into town as I had quite a bit of spare time before the Bradford bus left Keighley and as I was walking through, I met my granddaughters' husband. When I told him where I was going, he was horrified and insisted on taking me home immediately. He said that it had been advised that the authorities were anticipating civil disorder in Bradford, and on no account should I venture anywhere near there. I think he took me home because he was so worried, I might still go through to the city. When I put the news on the television that night, it was all about Bradford and the dreadful riots there. These riots lasted for quite some time, and I was certainly glad that I had been stopped from going. Apparently news of the expected trouble had been widely anticipated and I had been totally oblivious of it, but when I saw the news reports of the disturbances I thought that it was a good job that someone of my great age (I was then eighty-nine years old) had been prevented from being in the centre of it.

We also took lots of holidays and trips to occupy my mind and oh, the wonderful memories we had. Although they were not like our holidays to London during the war years, they were still brilliant, and I was happy to be a part of the memories of a new family, with my grandchildren.

One Summer I took the dog to *Flask Caravan Site* near Whitby. I stayed with her in Sylvia's caravan, a one bedroomed little thing they has towed there for me. Mavis and Edgar were staying there as well, and we managed to park next door to them. One day, Edgar and I started walking from Robin Hoods Bay and went to Whitby. It was a hard walk, taking the coastal path, but the three of us thoroughly enjoyed it. I think it was probably about a six-mile walk, but the dog probably walked twice as far as this. What a lovely day that was.

I went on quite a few holidays with my daughters and their families, and sometimes Daisy my sister came too. While my wife was alive, her sister Ivy and her husband would look after her to enable me to have a week's holiday. I spent a few happy holidays in Margate, and a memorable one in Northumberland, where I enjoyed visiting the Farne Islands. At that time, we were able to get off the boats and wonder round all three islands. I remember that it was nesting time for the Terns, and they were dive bombing us as we walked along. We also visited Lindisfarne – Holy Island, timing the tides right to cross to the Island so we didn't get stranded.

We also made many trips closer to home. On Tuesday nights – for a few month's when I was about eighty – we used to have a family trip to Cowling. There, we rented a small swimming pool for an hour and we would all go swimming. It was good time spent with family and teaching the youngsters how to swim. As well as the swim we enjoyed time in the sauna and the jacuzzi – both a first for me but I thoroughly enjoyed it.

In my later years, I have also enjoyed a number of exciting birthday parties, thrown by my family to celebrate my many milestone birthdays. I had never had a birthday party until I was sixty-five, and what a party that was! Then, I had another big party for my eightieth, it was a cabaret-type party where we were entertained whilst eating, alongside all my guests; my siblings, other family members and friends galore. I had another for my ninetieth as well, that party is clear in my memory. My daughters invited people to an afternoon party, and they had organised a concert type meeting. The songsters had learned my favourite song *'Moonlight and Roses'* and a favourite of my wife's, *'Deep Purple'*. Different people took part and I vividly remember the band accompanying Mavis to play a euphonium solo. A vivid memory because how many ninety-year-olds can accompany their daughter when she plays a solo. How lovely it was to have all my family and friends around me.

In 2004, unbeknown to me, one of my family contacted *Salvation Army Headquarters* in an attempt to get a surprise ninety-second birthday celebration card from the General of the *Salvation Army*. Unfortunately this was not possible due to time constraints and circumstances, however I received a very special Christmas card just a month later, with a personal message from General John Larsson, the 17th General of the *Salvation Army*, who held the position from September 2002 to April 2006; it read *"Brother George Harold Clough, I am delighted to learn that you are still going strong in the Lord's service. At ninety-two that must be something of a record! John Larsson"*. The *Keighley News* contacted me about this 'accolade' and, encouraged by my family and Keighley *Salvation Army Officers*, a reporter visited me, asked me some questions and then took a photograph of me in my *Salvation Army* uniform holding the card proudly aloft. The card depicted an artist's impression of St. Paul's Cathedral and the *Salvation Army's* new International Headquarters as seen from the Millennium Bridge at night. The newspaper article appeared in the Keighley News shortly after, and I felt a little like a novelty.

Unfortunately, as is the case in most tales, my later years were not filled entirely with happy stories. One of these incidents occurred on a trip to the Post Office to collect my pension. Having collected my pension, I caught the bus home and, on emptying my bag, I discovered my pension had been stolen! I was very upset and, to be honest, felt a little foolish.

Quickly though, I contacted the Department of Social Security and was assured that a new pension book would be sent to me. What did amaze me though was that they never asked if I could manage until I was able to get my next pension. Fortunately, I was alright, and I had a very helpful family who were always there for me, but I did wonder how some people would have coped who were less fortunate than me. There's no fool like an old fool, so the saying goes, and I proved this to be the case.

Some months later I was browsing the book section in the *Oxfam* shop on Keighley when a young man came up to me and asked if I could tell him what price it said in the book he was looking at. Always one to help people I looked in the book and was able to make out the price, told him and continued looking at the books. A few minutes later I realised the zip in my shopping bag was open and my pension book had gone. Fortunately, this time there was no cash with the book. After this I stopped putting my pension book in such a vulnerable place. In fact, soon after that I arranged with Sylvia for her to have it paid directly into her bank. These incidents did however make me realise that I was quite vulnerable.

I also began having difficulty with my eyesight and it was discovered that I had cataracts which needed removing. I had one eye done on the National Health Service and was told that there was to be a long wait for the second one. My daughters were not happy about this as, although it wasn't life threatening it was life limiting, and they felt waiting a few months when I was in my nineties was a long time. I couldn't see to play my music or to read so they decided that I had to have this operation privately. I do not want to seem as though I am criticising the National Health Service, but private patients are certainly treated differently.

For my first operation I was operated on and then moved to another waiting area where I was given tea and toast, before being checked and allowed home. It was fine but a bit like a production line. As a private patient the Consultant visited me at home to measure my lens. They phoned me the evening before my operation to check all was well for the next day. When I checked in at the hospital, I was shown to my own room to settle in. The Consultant came to check up on me, and then the porter came to take me to theatre. After my operation I was taken back to my room and served a meal. A couple of hours later I was visited once more by the Consultant and given dark glasses to wear. I later had a follow up appointment before being discharged. I know that there was nothing wrong with the NHS treatment, but as a paying patient I found the Consultant's manner totally different. What a marvellous operation this was. I could see again, and although I had worn glasses since I was twenty-one years old, I could manage without them now, but I was continually told I didn't look like me without them, so under pressure from my sister Kathleen I continued to wear them.

I have been fortunate enough never to suffer much illness in my life, and it was not until my nineties that things were beginning to go wrong with my health, but fortunately nothing serious. I developed a skin cancer which required an operation, it was a basal cell carcinoma, apparently the 'best' type to have if there is one, but still better to get rid of it. So, at this ripe age I had a 'face lift' as the removal of this cancer necessitated a cut from the side of my ear right down to my neck. It healed well and I haven't had any problems with it since.

As I said earlier, in March 1947 we came to live in the council house in Bracken Bank where I lived until 2005 and I was very happy there, but in 2005 I was finding a three bedroom house difficult to manage and my daughters suggested I moved to a flat. I applied to the Council to change my residence and due to my arthritis and my need for a walking stick to help me get around, the doctor backed my application. Within a month I had been offered a one bedroomed flat in Addingham. If I'm honest, I felt a little frightened to be moving after all the years I had lived at Bracken Bank. Of course, the family did all the cleaning and arranged the move, but I was moving to a new area, away from everything familiar. I had good neighbours where I was, they looked out for me to make sure I was alright. Anyway, I had worried needlessly for the move went well and I was happy there. The flat was in the village where Sylvia lived, and I linked up with Mount Hermon Church and spent a happy few years there. I was able to walk around the village and made many new friends. I even joined the choir at the chapel which I thoroughly enjoyed.

It was also around this time that Sylvia, Mavis, Edgar and I joined Silsden Town Band. It was a new experience for me because, prior to this, all my banding had been in the *Salvation Army*, so the music I was starting to play was vastly different. Initially, Ken the Musical Director put me on the third cornet part, but he soon approached me and asked me to move to the front row on solo cornet as he felt I would be more use there. This too, I thoroughly enjoyed and played with them until my health prevented me from doing so.

Keighley *Salvation Army* float in the Keighley Gala Procession in June 1977.

Me in 1990.

"On Duty"

Playing Christmas Carols in the Town
Centre December 1991. This sketch
of Mavis and myself was done by a
Brian, a friend of Mavis's while we
were playing to raise money for the
Christmas Appeal.

I've included this one as I never thought at that time that years later, I would be living here. Entertaining the residents in Currergate Nursing Home in 2000.

From left to right, Harry Dennis, Annie, Bernard, Ann, Me, Ada, Daisy, Kathleen and Linda. My surviving siblings on my eightieth birthday.

At Silsden Town Band.

Receiving my Long Service medal from Captain Len Evans.

My next move (and last move) was to Currergate Nursing Home, after surgery for an Abdominal Aortic Aneurism aged ninety-seven years. This kickstarted a completely different phase of my life.

I was extremely lucky to survive the Abdominal Aortic Aneurism. I had been in hospital for a few days, feeling very ill and having blood transfusions when, after a bad night, the doctors decided to do an endoscopy and discovered I had a massive bleed. They managed to seal the bleed without performing major surgery, but it was felt that I should go to a nursing home to recuperate. I have often wondered if this had been leaking all week and suddenly burst, as apparently in most cases this is fatal.

My room at Currergate was lovely, with a large bedroom and separate bathroom, and I must admit it was nice to be looked after. Although I managed quite well at home with the girls cooking for me and Sylvia doing my washing, I was finding it a little difficult as my knees were very painful and I used a walking stick. I was also developing a shake in my hands. I decided that I would give my flat up and move into the home. In truth, I didn't expect to be there very long.

I managed to occupy my time very well at Currergate. I was able to play my concertina in the home and spent many happy hours playing this and singing as well as using my mouth organ. One unfortunate turn of events was stopping playing my cornet as we were worried that the strain of playing could cause more problems with the aneurism. I had played for many years and I suppose I had done well continuing until this age, but I missed it dreadfully.

I recovered very well and didn't actually need nursing care, just someone to look out for me and cook my meals and make me drinks. They made it clear to me that this was my home, and as such, I was allowed the run of the home. I wondered around as and when I wanted, stayed in my room if I wanted or I would sit in the conservatory to play dominoes I spent a lot of my time visiting several of the other residents who were not as well as me and made some good friends. One particular friend loved football, but he had short term memory loss, and so often missed his favourite team playing when they were on television. I made a point of reminding him and would go to his room to put the television on so he didn't miss the programme. We also had some great entertainers, I particularly enjoyed it when Terry came along to sing.

Parties were always held for the different special occasions: St. Patricks Day, Christmas, Yorkshire Day and St. Georges Day and we had an annual Summer Fair, which my youngest great-grandchildren, Joshua and Charlotte loved to visit for! It was always my job to split the raffle tickets and then fold them ready for someone to pick out the numbers on the day. Raffles were organised for the Summer Fair, and at Easter and Christmas. All money raised was for the Patients Fund so that outings, parties and entertainment could be organised.

My family were always coming to visit with new and interesting things to keep my occupied. In November 2011, Dickie Bird, the Barnsley born test umpire visited Keighley to open a newly refurbished pub that had been named in his honour. As Dickie was born in the Staircross district of Barnsley, about three miles from my birthplace of Worsborough, Mark thought it would be fitting to give him a copy of my book at the event he was attending in Thwaites Brow. Later on, I received a signed copy of Dickie

Bird's autobiography for my birthday with a message from the retired umpire which read, 'To Harold Happy 99th Birthday "Ninety-nine NOT OUT" Best Wishes Dickie Bird'. It seemed we had swapped autobiographies! I wonder what Dickie thought of the 1997 version of my memoirs. Dickie Bird was approximately twenty years my junior, but grew up in the same area, briefly worked in coalfields (although not underground) and I'm sure he'd have had some similar experiences. Mark also provided me with a similar gift years later, from the comedy duo, The Grumbleweeds! A similar occurrence would happen again a few years later, when a member of the family visited Hebden Bridge where poet, writer and broadcaster Ian McMillan commonly referred to as 'The Bard of Barnsley' was re-opening a bookshop after the floods that hit the area in December and January. They returned with some presents for me various signed books of poetry and Yorkshire, however I also received a card from Ian with a bespoke poem he had written for me.

'It's very last minute at Wembley,
and Barnsley need a substitute,
and who's that coming on,
scoring with his left boot,
it's Harold the mystery striker,
all the way from STAIRFOOT'
All the best Ian McMillan

It seemed time was passing by quickly in my old age and before I knew it, I had reached the grand old age of one hundred! Imagine being alive for one hundred years, where had all the years gone?

The Sunday before my birthday, after the service at Chapel, there was a tea party to celebrate and they had made me a beautiful cake, decorated with musical notes and a small cornet.

At last the great day arrived. What celebrations we had that day, all which had been kept a total secret from me, but I remember every minute of that day as if it happened yesterday!

The day started with a visit from the family, including my sister Kathleen who was housebound. My grandson who lives in London had come up with his family. Then the postman came, and I had over a hundred cards, including one from the Lord Mayor of Bradford and a very special one from Her Majesty The Queen. In the afternoon there was a visit from the 'press' and I was interviewed and photographed by staff from The Keighley News. This was followed by a family party and Counsellor Keith Dredge (a family friend) attended on behalf of the Lord Mayor of Bradford. It was a great gathering and I thoroughly enjoyed it. I thought that was the end, but in the evening members of Silsden Town Band started arriving to do a concert just for me! The band played my favourite hymn tune and much of the music that I liked and had enjoyed playing. Sylvia also played a horn solo and Mavis played a solo on the Euphonium.

The concert was attended by many of my friends and, of course, my family. After the band had completed their programme, another buffet was served by the staff at Currergate. It really was a day to remember and, nothing was too much trouble for the staff at the home. There must have been about a hundred family and friends there at least, and they had all come just to wish me a Happy Birthday!

The evening programme was filmed, and so close family received DVD's as a keepsake of the event and a special video was done so that I could watch because I had never mastered the new-fangled DVD players. Family had paid tribute to me on the recording and it was lovely to listen to everything and everybody's good wishes.

At the beginning of January, after my one hundredth birthday, I began to feel unwell with a swelling in my groin. This turned out to be a strangulated hernia and I was rushed into hospital for surgery under a general anaesthetic. I think everyone thought that this would probably be the end for me as it was quite traumatic and a risk at my age, but within three days I was home again and at the end of a fortnight I was feeling back to my normal self. A hundred years old and I recovered fully within a few weeks.

Although I often sit and think about my home in Bracken Bank, I am happy at Currergate. I am fortunate to have many visitors and it is always nice to see old friends. I have also been visited regularly by a lovely man and his wife who live in the mews at the side of the home. I have always appreciated that people took the trouble to come and seem me.

I also like to occupy my mind with puzzles. I have always liked doing crosswords, and still try to complete the one in the newspaper every day. Sylvia buys the same paper, and I always like it if I've managed to finish it before her! Thinking of this reminds me of the time years ago when I had completed what I thought was a hard crossword in the paper. I don't remember the name of the paper, but I do remember that the prize for the first completed entry was a thousand pounds! I had finished it in record time, and decided to send my entry into the competition, leaving it with my Mum to post. Unfortunately, she forgot! It was indeed most unfortunate, because the money had been paid out to someone who had not completed it, they hadn't solved one of the problems. They paid out on a partially finished entry, because no one had sent a complete one in. Just imagine that, a thousand pounds, and what it would have meant to my family. Still, I suppose it wasn't to be.

I also got a lot of visits at the weekend from the younger ones in my family. Some Saturdays when my family visited the younger ones would sometimes ask me about the Second World War. I would recall my memories of hearing the wireless broadcasts of Adolf Hitler and how I was unnerved at the rise of the Nazi party. They would sing the World War Two song mocking the Nazi leaders, the lyrics were a little too rude for me to sing but Mavis, Mark and Charlotte took great delight in singing the following lyrics, to the tune of the 'Colonel Bogey March' in my bedroom. It was rather entertaining to say the least and although I don't swear, I chuckled when they launched into a rendition of this wartime 'classic'.

'Hitler has only got one ball
The other is in the Albert Hall
His mother, the dirty b*****
Cut it off when he was small
Hitler has only got one ball
Göring has two but very small
Himmler is rather sim'lar
But poor old Goebbels has no balls at all
She threw it into the apple tree
It fell into the deep blue sea

The fishes got out their dishes
And had scallops and b******* for tea'

It is true that life has been very different for me in these past few years, learning to accept being looked after in my old age. Sometimes, I feel to have wasted a lot of time over the last few years and have become lazy. I learned to knit when I was younger and often wonder if I should have taken this up once again as a useful hobby. I remember many years ago that Daisy decided to knit her Mother a cardigan for her birthday. It had been a very late decision and she was worried that she wouldn't complete in time to post it to London so that her Mum got it on the relevant day, so we made it a combined effort and Sylvia and I helped out with the knitting. We made a very good job of it even if I do say so myself.

The video recording machine has helped me wile away many hours. I particularly liked the series *'Last of the Summer Wine'* and *'Dad's Army'* and spent many happy hours watching these. I never tired of watching them and laughed at their antics every time. Unfortunately, in recent years I have had a lot of problems with arthritis in my knees and found that it was getting difficult to bend down to operate the machine, and I was frightened of falling, so the entertainment became unavailable to me. However, there are so many channels available on the television, all operable with a handheld remote control, that I've never been short of things to watch.

The other much-loved entertainment has been my C.D. player, which I can reach from my seat quite easily, so it is quite simple to operate. This has ensured that, although I was becoming less mobile, I never lacked entertainment, out of my large collection of singing artistes and brass band music.

Over the last few months I have been restricted to my room more and more due to the difficulty I have in walking, it has given me much time to think about my life and the state of the world. I have lived a very long life and in just over a hundred years I have seen many changes in the world. Travel in my young days was by horses, bicycles or walking as only the rich had cars, and of course there were boats and trains for people taking longer journeys. Nowadays households often have more than one car. I never learned to drive. Another missed opportunity? Probably as I did have the option to do so, but I don't think I've ever really regretted not learning. Now people travel all over the world, and in only a matter of hours, as the mode of travel used for most journeys to other countries is by aeroplane.

We used to be able to go out and leave our doors unlocked knowing all would be safe, mind you we didn't have much, but now things are much different, and we even lock our doors when we are sitting in our houses! I know that there have always been bad things happening in life, but I suppose one of the differences today is the media coverage which bring the details of everything into our living rooms.

How the world has changed since my birth and I suppose in a life that has spanned more than a century that is only to be expected. I'm glad to think not so many people will have to endure the poverty-stricken life I fought so hard to avoid for my own children.

Living accommodation has changed enormously for most people. Hot running water is the norm in the majority of houses, as are bathrooms which means there is no trek down the street now and no tin bath in front of the fire as there was in my childhood. But unfortunately, there are a large number of people in the country who are homeless and sleep out on the streets. The helping hand of the *Salvation Army* is just as necessary now as it was in my day. They now have programmes for feeding the homeless and run food banks for people who cannot afford to feed their families. A sad state of affairs in the twenty-first century. I was brought up in poverty and I could weep when I listen to the way the country is changing with people having to visit Food Banks so that they can feed their families, and the number of foodbanks that are springing up all over the country makes me think that many people are not much better off than we were back at the turn of the century!

I sit here and ponder what is happening in the world and do you know I don't really think things have changed in lots of ways, and certainly changes have not always been for the better. I have lived through two World Wars and yet I despair when I watch the news on the television and see the unrest throughout the world and the effects on the people and those poor children in the countries which are brought to life for us by the coverage of the television reporters. Refugees and Asylum Seekers as a result of war or political unrest are also part of the population of our country, as people flee from their own countries, often in the middle of the night as their lives are at risk, and these are also people who are helped today by the *Army*.

Radios became the norm in the 1930's and this changed our lives tremendously. We were able to sit in our own homes and listen to the news, not only from across the country but also the world. We would eagerly await the time for the stories. During the Second World War we would listen to the Prime Minister Winston Churchill uplifting broadcasts and our spirits would be raised. Then, in the late 1950's, television was introduced into the lives of the masses, as it became affordable for us to rent them. Black and white pictures originally, and if I remember correctly only one channel. In the 1960's another channel started broadcasting and this was followed by a second channel for the British Broadcasting Corporation, and even, colour television! Nowadays many of the youngsters don't bother with television, they download things onto their computers. They have computers they call tablets, in my day tablets were nothing more than medication! Imagine if I'd known any of these luxuries in my youth instead of breaking my back mining through the collieries under Barnsley!

While I have been writing my memoirs, it has brought to mind another change that I've seen, the invention of the *Biro* pen which I used to scrawl down my life memories. Prior to this we had to write using a fountain pen and ink, in fact often people wrote to each other using pencils to avoid the difficulties of fountain pens. Imagine the difference that this made to school children! In fact, when I went to school the children used to use chalk and a slate board.

Tape recorders were another brilliant invention I would have liked back in my youth, now we could record people speaking in our own homes on reels of special tapes.

These were soon superseded by the much smaller cassette recorders whereas before we had played records on record players (upgraded from wind ups to electric). Mentioning electric, what an invention that was when our houses were lit by electricity instead of gas. This also brought about other changes; out went the old flat iron which had to be heated over a grid on the fire, in came electric irons. The old, large ovens built into the fireplace were replaced by smaller less cumbersome gas or electric ovens. Video recorders came onto the scene and films could be rented, so people could watch them in their own homes. No need to go to the pictures, and it soon became possible to buy these films and tapes that could be used to record things from the television. These were then followed by the smaller DVD's, small circular discs about four inches in diameter. Then these were superseded by boxes supplied by broadcasting companies that record directly from the television, no tapes, cassettes or discs needed. With these gadgets you can even recall programmes you have missed.   A step too far for me in my old age!

The vacuum cleaner was a marvellous contraption when this came into our lives. Prior to this the floor covering had been cleaned using a dustpan and brush, but how easy the cleaning became with the introduction of the vacuum cleaner, even if compared to today's models, they were rather bulky and difficult to manoeuvre.

Air travel, of course, has made the world a much smaller place, as people now visit places I had only ever seen in an atlas. My own family have spent many holidays abroad, but I have never had the inclination to fly. To me, London is still the big and bright buzzing city it was when I was in my twenties.

I love Britain and have been quite content to visit various parts of my own country. My one regret is never going to Ireland. A few years ago, my daughters tried to persuade me to go there with them, but I refused, I felt that I had left it too late.

We had the telephone put into our house in the 1970's, Sylvia and Mavis insisted on this as they felt it was imperative that we were able to get help quickly if it was needed for either Daisy or myself. Some people did have them before this, but they were few and far between. Pay phones were largely relied upon and were in many of the streets in towns and villages, so it was easy for people to get in touch by phone, but they were rarely used as a social instrument, just for appointments, usually with the doctor or for other businesses. Now of course telephones are not the type that we had originally, a large black one with a dial to select the numbers. Not many people have landlines now, they all have mobiles and carry them around with them. These seem to do everything, I've seen people speak into them and ask them questions, and the answers pop up on the screen. Everyone seems to text each other now; no writing letters like in my day. If I'm honest I don't understand what they're writing, they seem to use another language. Though, how clever it is to be able to send photographs through these mobile gadgets. Another thing that I find incredible is that Mavis brings her computer, and videocalls with my great-granddaughter who is always travelling to far off places. Not only can I speak to her, but I can see her and she can see me. What an amazing invention! Then the other day, Charlotte used her phone to *FaceTime* her sister in South America, and we could speak and see each other on this small phone.   *Face Time*, I'd never heard of it.

I remember on my 80th birthday my sister-in-law Ivy saying to me *'You poor old sod, its all downhill from now'*. Well that's twenty-five years ago now and living to such a great age hasn't been bad at all. One great thing has been that not only have I been able to see my grandchildren grow up I have also been privileged to see my great grandchildren grow, I think this is a privilege that they feel is twofold in that they have been fortunate to be part of my life.

Well, I think that this just about completes the story of my life. I thought I hadn't long to live at my first tranche when I was a mere eighty-five years old, but now aged one hundred and five, I surely can't expect to be around much longer. I wrote the original story of my life by hand but haven't felt up to doing that for the rest of these memoirs but have dictated things to my daughter for her to include. I have added more things about my young life, for things have changed so much that these are part of our social history, and although some are a little sensitive, they were part of what happened to me, and made me into the person I am today. I have had a good life, a good 'innings'.

I have never known anybody of one hundred and five years old and often feel I am quite a novelty. I have a loving family who come to spend time with me. I have two daughters; they and their husbands are most helpful to me. I have three grandchildren and five great grandchildren. Yes! I am indeed fortunate and have had a good life so far. I still have two sisters alive, and me one hundred and five not out. Soon though

'I will be going on a journey
Not by jet plane or by car
Way beyond the utmost star
And my Lord will meet me there.'

My youngest grandson Mark had been discussing my memoirs with a young man who had written a book. This was an unusual book; it was not for sale but only able to be traded for something special to you. Mark had given him a copy of my original memoirs in exchange for this book.

Mike O'Brien was the young man's name and, after reading my thoughts he asked Mark if they could meet up and come to visit me. They both stayed a couple of hours and I had a lovely morning chatting to Mike. He wanted to know all about my life, what I'd seen and the things I'd done – I felt like quite the celebrity. A short time later he contacted Mark again, sending him a poem that he had written about me. I have added this at this part of my story with Mikes permission.

Open Door – Mike O'Brien

Pit days were hard, pit days were long, pit days were dark and damp
Pit days meant danger, risk and toil and up before the lark
Pit days meant walking miles between your house and your workplace
And more between the bottom of the shaft and the coal face
Pit days meant tiredness and dirt and aching limbs and back
And skin and hair no longer fair, but dirty, sore and black

When I worked down the pit I was not much more than just a boy
And time off work was precious time, to savour and enjoy
And one such time I found myself before an open door
And when I wandered through it, I was changed for evermore
I'd worked and lived in darkness up until that fateful night
But from that moment on things changed, I'd stepped into the light

I'd thought and talked of love and lasses many times before
But I didn't know a thing before I walked in through that door
Through that door I met the lass who would become my wife
She caught my eye and won my heart and turned around my life
What time I had to spend from that day on, it had to be
Spent next to her, no matter where, that's how it was for me

I'd heard my share of music too, and song before that day
But never understood how it can carry you away
Beyond that door, music took on significance for me
I learned to play; I trained my ear, listened voraciously
I joined a band, keen amateurs, devoted volunteers
I played the cornet in that band for years and years and years

I'd thought of matters spiritual before, I can't deny
Back then we all attended church, without much thought of why
But through that door I underwent some sort of transformation

I stood up for my beliefs and I was granted my salvation
It changed me inside and outside, I was awestruck and thrilled
Living in light, with love and music, happy and fulfilled

Pit days still hard, pit day's still long, pit days still dark and damp
But a light shone in me, brighter now than in my miner's lamp
And from that time, the perils of the pit could no more harm me
And soon I left and joined the ranks of the *Salvation Army*
A married man, a happy man with a long life ahead
I've lived a long, long time now, and know it's been a life well led

But, reading this you may think such a life is not for you
The things I've done are not the sort of things you want to do
And fair enough. I understand. To each his own I say
But I hope that love and light are there to guide you on your way
And if somehow, you feel they're not, don't give up, don't despair
Open your heart, open some doors, they could be anywhere

Farewell to the 'oldest citizen'

By Miran Rahman
miran.rahman@thegazette.co.uk

A MAN thought to be one of the oldest people in Keighley district has died, aged 105.

George Harold Clough, known as Harold, had been in Carrergate Nursing Home in Steeton for eight years, but previously spent half his life living in Bracken Bank.

His grandson Mark Clarkson, who lives in Keighley, said Harold died at the nursing home last month after a short illness.

"Almost until the end he was in very good health for his age, apart from a dodgy knee," he added. "He led a very active life when he was younger."

Harold's great granddaughter Charlotte Clarkson, said: "Despite being brought up in poverty, Harold lived a long and healthy life probably due to having not smoked since his early twenties, remaining teetotal throughout his life, being a keen walker, keeping his mind active and of course, his passionate faith."

Mark also attributed his grandfather's long life to his love of music. Harold was a keen singer, played the concertina, harmon-

Harold Clough, on his 105th birthday

ica and cornet and continued performing with Silsden Town band until he was 97. He sang in the choir until he was 98. Mr Clarkson said his grandfather continued playing the concertina even when he was over 100.

He was born in 1912 in Stairfoot, near Barnsley, the second eldest of 12 siblings. At the age of 14 he started work in the mines on the pit bottom where he was employed as a driver with a pit pony.

His job was to supply the older miners with tubs for them to fill with coal.

At the age of 21 he found himself out of work because younger boys were cheaper to employ on haulage in the mines.

Harold joined the Salvation Army in his early 20s, and it was there that he met and married lieutenant Daisy Richardson. He became a Salvation Army church leader in 1936.

Harold, Daisy and their first-born daughter Sylvia moved to Keighley in 1945, where they had another daughter Mavis. Harold lived in Elmwood Road, Bracken Bank, for 37 years until moving to Addingham in 2006.

During his working life Harold was a social driller at Widdop's Marine Engineering until the company moved to Scotland. He then worked at Sealand Engineering until his retirement.

He sang in the choir at the local Salvation Army for many years, and in the church choir at Mount Hermon Chapel when he lived in Addingham. By the time he stopped playing for Silsden Town Band he was the oldest brass band player in the UK.

Harold leaves his two daughters, two surviving sisters Annie and Daisy, three grandchildren and five great grandchildren. His funeral will be held at the Knowle, in Keighley, though a date has still to be confirmed.

News and disease travelled fast in 'Sodom', an estate at Stairfoot which had its heyday 100 years ago. Ian Thompson reports.

THE hanging out house walls would start with the tiniest bit of gossip in 'Sodom'.

People would then go to neighbours to listen to the news. This hom-less drum approach meant information travelled fast.

Noise played a big part in life at 'Sodom'.

On warm evenings, its streets would be a cacophony of sound as residents left their doors open and gramophones in each house played different tunes. Disease spread quickly too because everyone was so closely packed together.

Actor Michael Chance, who co-wrote 'Athersley and Stairfoot Revisited' with artist Tony Heald, said: "In the early days, Ardsley Urban District Council reports mention outbreaks of typhoid and scarlet fever.

"The homes were close together and there was poor sanitation."

'Sodom' was built in the late 1890s. Glasshouse Row on the corner of Stanley Road and Gregg's Row was the first of a group of what was to become about 100 homes in Hope Street, Industry Road, Alliance Road and Albion Road.

The homes were built to cater for an influx of people from Staffordshire, Lancashire and other parts of the country who came to work at Rylands Glassworks and the pits.

More than 500 people — or 80 families — virtually lived on top of each other.

No one is sure how 'Sodom' got its name. Girls and some outsiders were warned to avoid

Mr Heald believes it was something todo with the couldn't care less or 'sod 'em' attitude of those who lived there.

A typical home was two up, three down with cellars, a fireplace in the living room, a gas ring in the kitchen, a stone sink and flags on the floor.

There was no hot water, no baths. Water would be boiled on an open fire and men would wash off pit muck in a zinc bath.

Albion Road would be quagmire when it was wet because it was not surfaced in Tarmacadam.

"Sodom' had its wrong uns like anywhere else but during its heyday about a century ago people were cheerful, generous and warm-hearted.

"You learned early on to live on your wits."

An inspector was visiting Hunningley Lane School. He asked four boys — one of them from 'Sodom' — to take off their clothes except their trousers.

The lads were told to put their clothes on a pile and take five paces back. The inspector said he would give a shilling to the boy who dressed the fastest.

Inevitably, the 'Sodom' lad won. The boy had no buttons on his coat, shirt nor jumper and his shoes had no laces. All he did was throw his clothes back on.

In 1903, 'Sodom' came under the spotlight when a court considered if people had the right to use a footpath from Stanley Road to an off-licence.

Miner Albert Townsend, pit labourer William Hinchcliffe

and railman George William Nimsey were prosecuted for what we call criminal damage today.

It was alleged they had broken a fence, chain and door belonging to the off-licence owner Joseph Smith.

It was admitted the damage had been caused to obtain a right of way over a field owned by Mr Smith for the tenants of Bleachcroft Farm.

Several witnesses tried to prove there was no right of way but Thomas Harper, Ardsley Urban District Council's surveyor, said tenants of the farm had had a right of way for 60 years. Mr Harper said he had used the footpath many times.

The court believed Mr Harper and the case against Townsend, Hinchcliffe and Nimsey was dismissed.

'Sodom' was a happy hunting ground for the Salvation Army. The mission to save souls must have been successful as quite a few people from 'Sodom' attended Stairfoot Salvation Army Citadel.

A slum clearance programme in the 1960s did for 'Sodom' and its people.

Mr Chance said: "From what can remember, the houses looked pretty solid. Many of them had been converted knocked into two.

"It was a great pity the community was destroyed when they pulled the houses down.

"People from Sodom were split and moved to the big housing estates such as Kendray, Athersley and Lundwood."

Recently we discovered an article from the Barnsley Chronicle, entitled 'News and disease travelled fast in 'Sodom', an estate at Stairfoot which had its heyday 100 years ago. Ian Thompson reports. In this article Thompson puts forward a theory that Tony Heald co-writer of 'Athersley and Stairfoot Revisited' had suggested in relation to why the area was named 'Sodom', "Mr Heald believes it was something to do with the couldn't care less or 'sod'em' attitude of those who lived there".

A Final Farewell.

Majors Len and Ruth Evans, Officer friends of the family, travelled from Somerset to conduct the Funeral Service for Dad. It was a glorious summer day, when we said our last goodbyes to a much-loved man.

There were more than a hundred people there paying their last respects and celebrating a long and happy life. Mr Gordon Eddison, Musical Director of Silsden Town Band had organised with the band members to play for the Service and internment. The band was seventeen strong, with a couple from the *Salvation Army* Community Band and Keith Dredge, a family friend. Len started the Service with a touch of humour. Dad had always bought Sylvia and I, his great grandchildren and his sisters chocolate oranges, and Len handed pieces of chocolate oranges to everybody attending. Dads favourite songs were played by the band and sung by the congregation.

Sylvia and I paid tribute to Dad, his sister Daisy read the Bible and Georgina, Josie and Charlotte read the poem *'The Open Door'*. Francesca was in Australia but paid her tribute to him on the Order of Service. Lieutenant Ben Cotterill, Keighley Corps Commanding Officer also prayed during the Service.

In his lifetime Dad had sung many solos, one particularly beautiful song he sang at a friend's funeral – *'I am going on a journey'* – had been recorded by Sylvia and we decided that the only way for this celebration to end was by playing this recording. Charlotte made a DVD of this recording with photos of Dad with various people and this was shown before the Service ended.

We followed him to the cemetery where he was interred with Mum. The band accompanied the singing of *'God be with you till we meet again'*. We then moved on to Steeton Hall for a celebratory tea with all Dad's friends and family. Although it was a funeral, we had been careful to make sure it was actually a great celebration of his life, and many people came up to Sylvia and myself to say it was the best funeral they had ever been to.

A fitting farewell for a loved Father – Promoted to Glory 16th May 2018, laid to rest with Daisy, his wife.

Mavis Clarkson

Epilogue

The past is a different country?

I've just been to see my granddad & he had purchased a ticket/horse for the sweepstake where he lives, he then went on to tell me he didn't like the race would not be watching it, however if you'd have asked him the same question in the 1920's or in his teens he'd have been able to give you the full low down on weights, results, form for horses, jockeys & trainers. He then told us of a horse he'd tipped whilst in his teens, that he could not afford to back, but it won the Derby at odds of 100/6. The horse was called *April The Fifth*, (bit of a coincidence) & was raced in the name of Tom Walls who trained him at his stables at Epsom Downs. Although Walls had a keen interest in the sport he was much better known as a comic actor who was famous for his stage and film performances.

April The Fifth won the Derby in 1932, my granddad was nineteen, some eighty plus years ago. I have attached the follow information from *Wikipedia*.

'On 1 June, with a million spectators at Epsom Downs, April the Fifth started at odds of 100 to 6 (16.7/1) in a field of twenty-one runners with Orwell being made the 5/4 favourite, despite doubts concerning his stamina, ahead of the Newmarket Stakes winner Miracle. Ridden by Fred Lane, April the Fifth was restrained in the early stages before being produced with his challenge in the straight. Finishing strongly, he overtook the Aga Khan's colt Dastur inside the final furlong to win by three quarters of a length with Miracle a short head back in third. Firdaussi, the Aga Khan's other entry, finished fifth, while Orwell was ninth. The winning time was two minutes and 43 seconds. April the Fifth was a very popular winner and the first Epsom-trained horse to win the Derby since Amato in 1838. After the race, Walls joked that he would consider changing the horse's name from "April the Fifth" to "June the First".'

Mark Clarkson

Our Memories

A short collection of memories about a man we loved.

'I used to come up from London every year for his birthday, and when it came to his one hundredth, he had saved all his cards for me to open with him. It made me feel so special and loved and just demonstrates what a thoughtful and caring man he was.' **Josie.**

'I will never forget how Georgina; my niece had once asked how old he was at one of his birthday parties. After he replied, she said to him, 'You will get dead next!' and he couldn't stop laughing. We talked about that for years to come and it would always give him a chuckle.' **Kirsty.**

'I loved Wednesday nights at Harold's house. We would go over for tea and darts and would talk about Barnsley. I was only six when we moved, but still had so many memories of it and Harold was the only one who could share in these. I also remember another occasion where Harold and Daisy, home on holiday bought me two Shirley Temple dresses as a surprise and how happy I was! They were always treating me, in fact, they were the ones to buy me my first New Testament Book. I think of him often, especially whenever I hear Moonlight and Roses.' **Annie.**

'Being in Cleethorpes always reminds me of Uncle Harold as he and Auntie Daisy would come over every year and stay with us for their holidays. We used to have great fun when we were kids, when they both came, and I always admired Uncle Harold and how he looked after Auntie Daisy and did everything for her. He used to take her to Cleethorpes a lot as it was her favourite place. I remember him pushing her up a big hill every time because, for him, nothing was ever too much trouble. Uncle Harold was a lovely man and I have some very fond memories of him. He lived life to the full.' **Julie.**

'My favourite memories are of his made-up song, "Ooo long glisky wolla wolla whisky" and his amazing stew and dumplings with giant Yorkshire puddings! I also remember how he would cobble my shoes.' **Sharon.**

'He was a wonderful man and Len absolutely loved his baking. I used to enjoy making beds with him on a Saturday afternoon when I lived with them... it's the little things.' **Joan and Len.**

'Thinking of Gramps makes me think of his kindness and how he would walk through Currergate, despite being one of the oldest residents there, to visit other residents and help brighten their spirits.' **Joshua.**

'There are so many lovely memories I have with him, but one that stands out is being with him in the Lake District to attend Sharon's wedding. He was nearly ninety, but arrived, fresh as a daisy and did a lovely reading in service. Treasured memories.' **Sylvia.**

'Ever one for a crossword, Gramps, Mum and I were trying to find the final few missing answers to the Daily Mail crossword. After much deliberation, we needed to check if the

letters partially making up the missing answers were correct. We asked Gramps what the word was, and he said 'place-bow', (placebo). My Mum and I looked at each other, confused, then had a look ourselves, the word was 'pluh-see-bow' (placebo), we all laughed so much, Gramps even managed to take a funny turn. Anyway, after that I used to visit him and without fail, every time I was about to leave, I would say keep taking the 'place-bow'.' **Mark.**

'I have lovely memories of going shopping with Harold. We would often go to Bradford and look round the charity shops there. Harold was a great one for picking up books. We would then go into a café in the market to have our dinner.' **Daisy.**

'He used to love walking and I have happy memories of the many hikes we went on together. When the boys were younger, they would come with us, and whenever Ralph was over on holiday, he would join us too.' **Edgar.**

'One incident that has caused much laughter over the years happened whilst Dad was decorating the bathroom. We had a wooden chair in the corner of the bathroom, and he had painted this and put it into the dining room to dry. I had come into the house with a friend, Eric Smith, so as not to disturb my parents, we went into the dining room to chat. Dad had warned us about the chair being painted and not to touch it and we were careful not to. But, a while later he wanted something form the sideboard in the dining room. He opened the drawer and sat down to look in it and you've guessed it, he had sat down on the wet chair!' **Mavis.**

'When I think of Gramps its usually in his house at Bracken Bank where I spent many happy hours with him.' **Nigel.**

'I remember the times when he used to stay with us in Cleethorpes and we would watch Wimbledon with him.' **Ann.**

'Making pies in the kitchen, and him letting me make my own mini pie. He even bought me my own mini rolling pin.' **Francesca.**

'A conversation with him on his 103rd birthday. I was in Australia and Grandma had taken the laptop to him so that I could speak to him. He was so in awe that we could speak over such a long distance, he said 'It's a miracle'. He said that he had never been on a plane. I told him I could see him as clear as day, as if he was there in Australia with me. Then I remember the last time I saw him. He took mine and Charlottes hand from his bed and said, 'take care love.' **Georgina.**

'Stickability is a word I associate with him. The way he would never be beaten by the weekend crossword puzzle, often ringing during the week when he solved a real toughie! Typical of him not to be beaten.' **Barry.**

Glossary

1. Last - used by cobblers when mending shoes. It is made from cast iron and shaped tripod like on three different sized feet. The cobbler chooses which is the best size foot for the shoe he is mending, places the shoe on this so that it is on the top of the last and the last rests on the other two feet. This enables the cobbler to have his hands free to work on the shoe.
2. Donkey-stoning – steps and ledges would be washed with water and then coloured with a white or yellow ochre donkey-stone.
3. Ston o bread - stone of bread, a stone was fourteen pounds. To make a stone of bread a stone of flour was used.
4. Midden – a waste piece of ground where people used to tip their rubbish, usually ashes from the fire. There was a grid on the ground which allowed the ashes to go through and onto the ground below, where the earth closets were dug out.
5. Middy Man – a dustbin man employed by the council who would often see to clearing out the debris from the earth closets.
6. Bit – a slang term for a person's wages.
7. Allotments – a plot of land where people could grow flowers or vegetables. These were usually rented from the council, as very few people had gardens attached to their houses in those days.
8. Dripping – the fat left after a joint of meat had been cooked.
9. Charabangs – a form of transport; similar to a tram, Charabangs had four or five rows of seats, each holding six people with separate doors to each row.
10. Trackies – slang term for buses as they did not run on rails like trams or trains.
11. Dab hand – proficient.
12. Spanish – a Yorkshire slang term for liquorice.
13. Tick – on credit.
14. Cage – a sort of lift to take people from one floor of the mine to another.
15. Driver – the person in charge of a pit pony or cart horse.
16. Nip – an interchangeable nickname between Willie and I.
17. *Dante's Inferno* – a fourteenth century epic poem 'Divine Comedy' where the author journey's through Hell.
18. Corporal – the man in charge of a certain mining district and therefore is in charge of the district's drivers by default.
19. Manhole – a recess made in the side of a tunnel so men could get inside and allow the tubs to go by unhindered, such recesses were spaced every hundred yards or so.
20. Snap – sandwiches taken for lunchbreak.
21. Drifters – men who were drilling and blasting their way through rock and stone on a new coal face.
22. Britching – turning around in a small, confined space.
23. Paddy – a thirty-ton *Chevrolet* lorry with forms placed down each side of the back and protected from the weather by a canvas cover.
24. Half a crown – twelve and a half pence in modern day currency.
25. Corps – *Salvation Army* terminology for a group where they worship.
26. Open Air – a meeting held by Salvationists in the open street.

27. Poker Work Motto – text burnt into wood with a poker.
28. Candidate – a term used in the *Salvation Army* for someone who has applied to be an Officer and is waiting to attend the training college.
29. Cadet – a person attending the training college.
30. Field Training – learning how to conduct meetings, this was practiced at the Corps adjoining the College which was, in my case, Battersea and Wandsworth (a Young People's Training Corps) and Westminster.
31. Hansom cab – a horse-drawn carriage.
32. Self-Denial – this was a period in the *Salvation Army* calendar when people were asked to deny themselves so that they could give money to the poor, in this country and abroad. As well as asking Salvationists to give money, the Salvationists collect from members of the public in what is termed door to door collecting. This, as the term suggests, is knocking on each door in an area.
33. Commissioning day - the day the cadets were appointed as Salvation Army Officers.
34. Cornet – a brass musical instrument.
35. Concertina – a musical instrument, played by holding in both hands and pulling and closing the bellows. The sound is made by free vibrating reeds on metal.
36. Quarters – a house provided by the *Salvation Army* for their officers to live in.
37. Divisional Commander – officer in charge of an area which contained several corps. This person did not look after a corps.
38. Scrubology – a term used when a group of people meet together to clean a building. It is a term and indeed a practice still used in Churches and *Salvation Army* Citadels today.
39. Eventime home – home for the elderly.
40. Pub booming – selling *Salvation Army* publications to public house customers.
41. Doodlebugs – The Luftwaffe's V-1 flying bomb used against the Allies and dropped throughout south-east England.
42. Tandem bicycle – a bicycle with two seats, one behind the other so that two can ride the same bicycle.
43. Songsters – A choir.
44. Home League – Ladies meetings.
45. Coke – a derivative of coal, a process removes all the gas from the coal. It is a smokeless fuel.
46. Citadel – the hall where our *Salvation Army* services were held.
47. Wind Up - another meeting of singing, testimonies and pieces played by the band and songs from the songsters.
48. Posser - a copper bell shaped implement with holes in which was fitted on a wooden pole.
49. Washboard – a corrugated piece of galvanised steel set into a wood frame for ease of holding.
50. Corps Cadet Guardian - the leader of a Bible study group for teenagers.

Printed in Poland
by Amazon Fulfillment
Poland Sp. z o.o., Wrocław